ECDL Module 2:
Using the Computer and Managing Files

Springer
London
Berlin
Heidelberg
New York
Barcelona
Hong Kong
Milan
Paris
Singapore
Tokyo

ICDL Approved Courseware
Syllabus Version 3.0

ECDL Approved Courseware
Syllabus Version 3.0

ECDL Module 2: Using the Computer and Managing Files

ECDL – the European PC standard

 Springer

BCS

The Publisher and the BCS would like to publicly acknowledge the vital support of the ECDL Foundation in validating and approving this book for the purpose of studying for the European-wide ECDL qualification.

Springer-Verlag London Ltd, Sweetapple House, Catteshall Road, Godalming, Surrey GU7 3DJ or

The British Computer Society, 1 Sanford Street, Swindon, Wiltshire SN1 1HJ

ISBN 1-85233-443-6

British Library Cataloguing in Publication Data
Penfold, David
  ECDL module 2: using the computer and managing files: ECDL – the European PC standard. – (European computer driving licence)
  1. Microcomputers
  I. Title
  004.1'6

  ISBN 1852334436

The use of registered names, trademarks etc. in this publication does not imply, even in the absence of a specific statement, that such names are exempt from the relevant laws and regulations and are therefore free for general use.

Disclaimer
Although every care has been taken by the author, the British Computer Society and the Publisher in the preparation of this publication, no warranty is given by the author, the British Computer Society and the Publisher as to the accuracy or completeness of the information contained within it and neither the author, the British Computer Society nor the Publisher shall be responsible or liable for any errors or omissions.

Printed and bound at The Cromwell Press, Trowbridge, Wiltshire, England.
34/3830-543210 Printed on acid-free paper SPIN 10792497

Preface

This book is intended to help you successfully complete the test for Module 2 of the European Computer Driving Licence (ECDL). However before we start working through the actual content of the guide you may find it useful to know a little bit more about the ECDL in general and where this particular Module fits into the overall framework.

What Is The ECDL?

The European Computer Driving Licence (ECDL) is a European-wide qualification that enables people to demonstrate their competence in computer skills. It certifies the candidate's knowledge and competence in personal computer usage at a basic level and is based upon a single agreed syllabus.

This syllabus covers a range of specific knowledge areas and skill sets, which are broken down into seven modules. Each of the modules must be passed before the ECDL certificate can be awarded, though they may be taken in any order but must be completed within a three year period.

Testing of candidates is at audited testing centres, and successful completion of the test will demonstrate the holder's basic knowledge and competence in using a personal computer and common computer applications.

The implementation of the ECDL in the UK is being managed by the British Computer Society. It is growing at a tremendous rate and is set to become the most widely recognised qualification in the field of work-related computer use.

The ECDL Modules

The seven modules which make up the ECDL certificate are described briefly below:

Module 1: Basic Concepts of Information Technology covers the physical make-up of a personal computer and some of the basic concepts of Information Technology such as data storage and memory, and the uses of information networks within computing. It also looks at the application of computer software in society and the use of IT systems in everyday situations. Some basic security and legal issues are also addressed.

Module 2: Using the Computer and Managing Files covers the basic functions of a personal computer and its operating system. In particular it looks at operating effectively within the desktop environment, managing and organising files and directories, and working with desktop icons.

Module 3: Word Processing covers the use of a word processing application on a personal computer. It looks at the basic operations associated with creating, formatting and finishing a word processing document ready for distribution. It also addresses some of the more advanced features such as creating standard tables, using pictures and images within a document, importing objects and using mail merge tools.

Module 4: Spreadsheets covers the basic concepts of spreadsheets and the ability to use a spreadsheet application on a personal computer. Included are the basic operations for developing, formatting and using a spreadsheet, together with the use of basic formulas and functions to carry out standard mathematical and logical operations. Importing objects and creating graphs and charts are also covered.

Module 5: Database covers the basic concepts of databases and the ability to use a database on a personal computer. It addresses the design and planning of a simple database, and the retrieval of information from a database through the use of query, select and sort tools.

Module 6: Presentation covers the use of presentation tools on a personal computer, in particular creating, formatting and preparing presentations. The requirement to create a variety of presentations for different audiences and situations is also addressed.

Module 7: Information and Communication is divided into two main sections, the first of which covers basic Web search tasks using a Web browser and search engine tools. The second section addresses the use of electronic mail software to send and receive messages, to attach documents, and to organise and manage message folders and directories.

This guide focuses upon Module 2.

How To Use This Guide

The purpose of this guide is to take you through all of the knowledge areas and skill sets specified in the syllabus for Module 2. The use of clear, non technical explanations and self paced exercises will provide you with an understanding of the key elements of the syllabus and give you a solid foundation for moving on to take the ECDL test relating to this Module. All exercises contained within this guide are based upon the Windows 98 operating system and Office 97 software.

Each chapter has a well defined set of objectives that relate directly to the syllabus for the ECDL Module 2. Because the guide is structured in a logical sequence you are advised to work through the chapters one at a time from the beginning. Throughout each chapter there are various review questions so that you can determine whether you have understood the principles involved correctly prior to moving on to the next step.

Conventions Used In This Guide

Throughout this guide you will come across notes alongside a number of icons. They are all designed to provide you with specific information related to the section of the book you are currently working through. The icons and the particular types of information they relate to are as follows:

information

Additional Information: Further information or explanation about a specific point.

caution!

Caution: A word of warning about the risks associated with a particular action, together with guidance, where necessary on how to avoid any pitfalls.

definition

Definition: A plain English definition of a newly introduced term or concept.

shortcut

Short Cuts: Short cuts and hints for using a particular program more effectively.

As you are working through the various exercises contained within this guide, you will be asked to carry out a variety of actions:

● Where we refer to commands or items that you are required to select from the PC screen, then we indicate these in bold, for example: Click on the **Yes** button.
● Where you are asked to key text in to the PC, then we indicate this in italics, for example: Type in the words '*Saving my work*'.

You should now be in a position to use this guide, so lets get started. Good luck!

Contents

★ ★ ★
★ ECDL ★
★ ★ ★

Introduction

In this chapter we will

- *Give a little history of the PC.*
- *Give a brief outline of how file structures work.*
- *Give a brief introduction to the use of windows and icons.*
- *Explain the structure of the rest of the book.*

1.1. Introduction

The first module of the ECDL is all about information technology in general. In this module we look at how to use the computer, in this case what is referred to as the PC, and how to manage your files.

1.2. A Little Bit of History

PC stands for personal computer and what we generally call PCs today are based on the PC first developed by IBM in about 1980. Before long other companies began to manufacture and sell similar machines, generally built around an Intel processor and first called clones, but more recently referred to as IBM-compatible computers. These are the computers that the majority of people and businesses use on their desktops, although there are other systems, most notably the Apple Macintosh, which is also a personal computer, although, perhaps rather confusingly, not usually referred to as a PC. The Mac, as it is generally known, has a very loyal following and is widely used in the graphic arts industries.

When IBM started to develop the PC, they selected a small software company called Microsoft to design the operating system, which, put simply, is the software that allows the user to interact with the processor using a series of commands in something like natural language. They called this operating system PC-DOS (DOS = disk operating system). Subsequently, IBM and Microsoft parted ways and the operating system was then called MS-DOS (and often just DOS). DOS went through a number of versions, but it remained what is called a command-line interface, so that to carry out any operation, you have to type a command followed by the return key. An example of a DOS screen is shown in Figure 1.1.

Figure 1.1 DOS screen with command-line interface.

Then in the mid-1980s, Apple developed the Mac, which had what is called a graphical user interface, using windows, icons and a mouse. How much this influenced Microsoft was the subject of several court cases, but, at about the same time Microsoft developed the first version of Windows, which has itself gone through a number of versions, the latest of which is Windows 2000. However, as Windows 2000 is very new, this guide focuses upon Windows 98, which, along with Windows 95, is still widely used. In general, Windows 95 is very similar to Windows 98, but where there are significant differences, they will be pointed out. Note that, although people still write programs for which you need to use DOS, all the major commercial software is now written for Windows consequently for all the software discussed in this and subsequent modules, you only need to know about Windows. Windows 95 and later versions are operating systems in their own right, whereas earlier versions, of which Windows 3.1 was the last, were effectively programs run from DOS, so it was important to understand the relationship between the two. Here we mention DOS for completeness. Although you can open a DOS window in Windows 98, you can access all the information you need to know from within Windows.

Finally, you may also hear of operating systems called Unix and Linux. These can be run on PCs, but are beyond the scope of ECDL.

1.3. Filing and File Structures

There are two common ways of looking at how files are organised in Windows (and, in fact, on every common operating system). The metaphors used are the filing cabinet and the inverted tree. Figure 1.2 shows the filing cabinet, so that you can think of the whole of your system as the cabinet. Then each disk (or partition on a disk) is effectively a drawer and these are labelled. A: is the diskette (or floppy disk) drive, C: the main hard drive and D: or E: the CD drive. (B: may be used for a second diskette drive, often a 5.25-inch drive, and D: is now often used for a removable drive such as the Iomega Zip drive.) Within each of these 'drawers' are large files called directories or folders. Any directory can contain either other directories or individual files (such as programs or application files, for example word-processing or spreadsheet files) and effectively you can have as many levels of directory as you wish. As we shall see, it is wise to use a logical structure so that it is easier to find your files!

Figure 1.2 Windows uses cabinet and folder metaphors for filing.

The other metaphor is an inverted tree (see Figure 1.3). Here your system level is called the root (and in the Unix operating system, this is what the top-level directory is indeed called), although perhaps trunk would have been more apt. Each directory can then be thought of as a branch and each individual file as a leaf. It really does not matter which metaphor you use, as long as you understand the idea of files within directories within other directories and so on.

Root

Figure 1.3 The inverted tree metaphor can be used for filing.

Self Study

Draw a directory structure for your ECDL studies. At the top put ECDL and then provide a directory or folder for each module. Within each module, you could perhaps have directories for notes and for exercises. See if there are any other directories that may be useful.

1.4. Windows and Icons

When you open a window (and we shall see how to do this), it represents either a directory or an individual file. When you open a window representing a directory, you will see icons (or possibly the names of files) within that window which represent either other directories or individual files (see Figure 1.4). If you try to open an individual file, one of two things can happen. If the file is a program (an application, such as Word 97, for example), then the application will open in its own window. If, however, you try to open a file that is not a program, then once again one of two things can happen. If the file is associated with an application (for example, it is a Word 97 word-processing document), then the file will open in the window of that application. If there is no such association, then you will be asked what application you want to use. This is really outside the scope of ECDL, but is useful to know.

Figure 1.4 Icons representing files appear within an open window.

Icons, thus, represent files or directories, at least when they appear on what is called the desktop, which is the view of your system that you get before you open up any applications.

1.5. Outline of the Guide

In Chapter 2, we look the basic use of the computer:

● How to start the computer, how to restart it and how to shut it down properly.
● The Windows 98 user interface options.
● How to look at basic system information, i.e. to see what your system consists of.

- How to look at basic desktop information, such as screen settings, the time and date and other options.
- How to format a diskette (floppy disk). Note that formatting a hard disk is not covered within ECDL.
- How to use Help functions. Your system has extensive help built into it and being able to use this properly is really important and often overlooked. If you can find the information you want by using Help, then using your computer will seem a whole lot easier. Incidentally, although not covered in ECDL, we shall also note what to do when the system or an application 'freezes'.

In Chapter 3 we shall look at icons, not only how to select and move them, but also how to recognise basic types of icon, such as directories and applications. We shall also learn how to create what is called a shortcut.

Chapter 4 will be about windows (with a small w). We shall learn:

- How to recognise the different parts of a desktop window.
- How to reduce, enlarge, minimise and close a window.
- How to recognise the aspects that all application windows generally have in common.
- How to move between windows and between applications.

The next three chapters are about file structures and file handling. First, in Chapter 5 we shall go into detail about file and directory structures and then we shall see the following:

- How to create directories and subdirectories.
- How to view the properties of a directory.
- How to recognise different types of icons representing files and how to view the properties of these files.
- How to rename files and directories.

In Chapter 6 we shall see look at selecting, copying, moving and deleting files and directories, including making copies to a diskette.

Chapter 7 is about using the Find tool to locate a file or directory. We shall also see how to use different properties of a file to locate it.

Chapter 8 is concerned with editing text files. Although we shall look briefly at word processing, this is dealt with in detail in Module 3. Here we shall look at:

● Launching an editing program or word processor.
● Opening a file or creating one and saving it.
● Closing the file and the application.

Finally, Chapter 9 is about printing, changing the default printer and viewing the progress of a print job.

The guide concludes with an index.

Summary

In this chapter:

● We have seen some the background to the PC and to Windows.
● We have seen how files are organised.
● We have seen how windows and icons are used.
● We have looked at an outline of the remainder of the guide.

★ ECDL ★

First Steps with the Computer

In this chapter you will learn how to

- *Start the computer.*
- *Restart the computer.*
- *Shut down the computer.*
- *Utilise the Windows 98 user options.*
- *Adjust the desktop.*
- *Find system information.*
- *Find basic desktop information.*
- *Find information about your disks.*
- *Format a diskette/floppy disk.*
- *Use Help functions.*

2.1. Introduction

This chapter is rather long, so you may find it easier to consider it in three sessions, the first concerned with starting the computer, finding out about Windows 98 desktop view options and the desktop itself. In the second session, you can look at finding and changing system information, while in the third session you can experiment with Help.

2.2. How to Start the Computer, How to Restart It and How to Shut It Down Properly

Obviously, the first thing you need to be able to do is start your computer and understand what is happening when you do.

We will assume that you have connected everything up correctly or that someone else has done this for you. If in doubt, consult the manual or someone with experience. Today, when most PCs are sold as boxes, consulting your supplier may not be a very helpful approach.

Exercise 2.2

In most, but not all, cases, the various components of the system have separate switches, so you need to power on the monitor (screen), the speakers and any other peripherals, for example an external Zip drive, before you switch on the computer itself. Incidentally, while it is probably a good idea to switch on a scanner or a printer at the same time, this is not usually essential, because they will work satisfactorily if you switch them on later. This is, in fact, usually true of the monitor and speakers as well, but, certainly as far as the monitor goes, there is little point in switching on the computer if you cannot see what is happening on the screen!

When you switch on, you will initially see a basic screen display of (usually) white characters on a black background. What this is telling you is that the system is running a series of checks on your hardware and the system software, some of which is stored on Read-only Memory (ROM) chips and the rest on the hard disk of your computer. You can intervene at this point to make changes, but this is outside the ECDL syllabus and it is recommended that you do not do so without expert advice or until you have learnt more about the system.

If all is well, then eventually you will see a Windows 98 introductory screen, followed in due course by the Windows 98 desktop. How long this will take –

perhaps as long as a few minutes, but probably less for a new system –
depends on various factors, such as the speed of your processor and how
many programs have been set up to start automatically when you switch on.
The latter can also be changed by you, but again is outside the ECDL
syllabus. Figure 2.1 shows a typical desktop. We will look at this in the next
section, but note that when you first use your computer, you will usually see a
window that offers you the opportunity to find out more about Windows 98. If it
does not appear as shown in Figure 2.1, then you can open it from the Start
button at the bottom left of the screen. Click **Start** with your left mouse button
and then select **Programs**, then **Accessories**, then **System Tools** and
finally **Welcome to Windows**. Note that you need to have the Windows 98
CD in your CD drive to access the information available from this screen (or
the information needs to be loaded somewhere on your network if you are
working on a network – ask the helpdesk or the system administrator if you
have a problem).

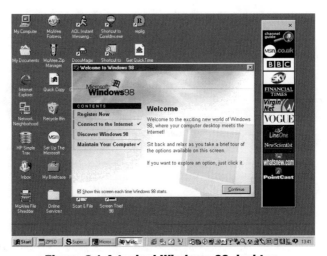

Figure 2.1 A typical Windows 98 desktop.

It is a good idea to follow the trails from this introductory window before you
start to use the system. They will overlap to a certain extent with what we talk
about here, but should make matters easier to understand. You will note that
you are given the option to start at your own knowledge level, which is good.
Most people reading this book will want to start at the basic level.

Self Study

Spend some time following through the various trails in Discover
Windows 98, starting at a level that is appropriate for yourself.

To restart your computer or to close it down involves very similar operations. In either case it is a good idea to close down all the applications you are running before you move to restart or close down. If you do not, then there may be various effects:

● You will probably see a series of prompts asking you if you want to save files you have been working on if they are still open.
● You may see a message saying that an application is still running, giving you the option of waiting or cutting short its operation and possibly losing changes.
● Finally, when you start the computer again, you may find that some of the windows you had open when you closed down have re-opened automatically, which you may not want.

So, close all the programs you can see on your desktop before you shut down.

Once you have closed applications in the usual way (and we will look at the end of this section into how to close down an application that is not responding), you click on the **Start** button (in the bottom left corner of the screen. Then click **Shut Down** and a window will appear in the centre of the screen asking what you want to do (see Figure 2.2). If you want to shut down the computer, then click the appropriate button and then watch the screen until either you see a message telling you that it is safe to switch your computer off or the system switches your computer off automatically; different systems work in different ways. You may also have to turn off the monitor and any peripherals, depending whether they operate from separate power supplies or not – most do.

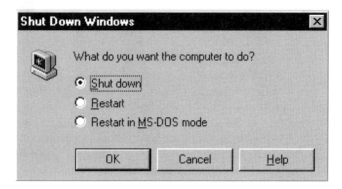

Figure 2.2 Message that appears when closing your computer down.

If, instead of shutting down, you want to restart your computer, then again you click the appropriate button and the system will go through the same shut-down procedure as for shutting down. However, this time it will then go through the start-up procedure, just as if you had switched off and switched on again.

Self Study

Restart your computer and watch the screen as it goes through all its initial tests.

Why should you want to restart? There are two main reasons:

● You have installed new or updated software and it is necessary for the computer to be restarted for the software to be usable or the updates to be effective. In fact, this restart may be part of the installation procedure, although you are always asked whether you want to restart and asked to confirm.
● An application is not working as it should; this unfortunately still happens. In such a situation, restarting can often solve the problem, because essentially you are exiting from the problem situation. At the end of this section we will look at what to do if an application 'freezes', i.e. does not respond to the mouse or the keyboard.

2.3. The Windows 98 User Interface Options

Although this is not strictly part of the ECDL syllabus, unless you understand how to use and possibly change the user interface to what suits you best, you may not find yourself as comfortable with your computer as is desirable.

Windows 95, the predecessor to Windows 98, only offered one interface option or view, referred to as the Classic style. It shows how fast things change in this area that a style can become a classic in only a few years; the first version of Windows only appeared about ten years ago, but the interface changed quite significantly with Windows 95, so it has become 'classic' in only three years! Windows 98 offers you three options, the Classic view, the Web view, and the Custom view. You choose which view by using the menu **Folder Options** (Figure 2.3), accessed from the **Start** menu and by then choosing **Settings** and then **Folder Options**:

Figure 2.3 Folder Options offers the three interface options.

● **The Classic view:** We shall look at this first because it is easier to see what is different in the Web View if you understand the Classic view. In the Classic view, Directories (see Sections 1 and 5) appear as shown in Figure 2.4. Applications and application files appear as an appropriate icon, while sub-directories (sub-folders) appear as an icon that looks rather like an index card. To select a file or directory, you click once with the left mouse button. To open the sub-directory or file or to start an application, you either click again on the selected icon or you double click on a previously unselected icon.

Figure 2.4 Directories as they appear in the Classic view.

● **The Web view:** Module 7 on Information and Communication includes sections on the Internet and the World Wide Web (often referred to as the Web or WWW). Microsoft's web browser is called Internet Explorer (IE) and Windows 98 is integrated much more closely with IE than Windows 95 was. For example, on your Windows desktop (see Figure 2.1) you may see a panel showing channels that you an access by just clicking on them (if, of course, you have a connection to the Internet). We shall not be talking about the Internet or the Web here, but what is important is that the Web view of your desktop uses the same approach to accessing files and programs as IE does. What this means is that instead of looking like Figure 2.4, a window looks like Figure 2.5. Now to select an icon (and in general the icons tend to be more descriptive), you just have to move the cursor over it (this is called 'mousing over') and, to activate or open it, you click just once. This is how you select and open on a Web page.

Fugure 2.5 Viewing the desktop using the Web view.

● **The Custom view:** The Custom view, as you might expect, allows you to choose how you view the desktop (see Figure 2.6). It effectively allows you to 'mix and match'. However, at this stage, we suggest that you choose either the Classic view or the Web view (perhaps switching between them, which you can do at any time, to see which one you prefer). If, once you are familiar with the two main views, you want to customise, then that is fine. Note that, in switching views, you are only changing how you look at the information and data on your computer. You are not affecting that information and data at all, so you can change views as often as you wish.

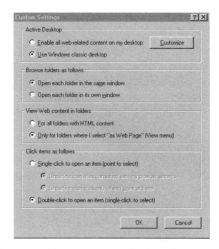

Figure 2.6 Users can select their preferred desktop using the Custom view.

We shall point out any differences between Windows 95 and Windows 98 as we go.

Self Study

Consider the differences between the two standard views of the desktop and examine some of the custom options. What is your initial reaction? Which desktop view do you prefer? Discuss with your colleagues if possible.

information

> **Clicking: Throughout the book, we shall refer to clicking with the left mouse button simply as 'clicking', while clicking with the right mouse button we shall refer to as 'right clicking'. In the classic view, a single click (with the left button) selects and a double click opens; in the Web view, passing the mouse over an icon selects it and clicking opens. Right clicking almost always opens a floating menu, the contents of which will depend on the application being used and, indeed, where the cursor is in that application. If you have a three-mouse button, clicking the central mouse button changes the scroll bar (within applications), so that you can scroll smoothly. You may also have a wheel that you can scroll with.**

information

Although this book is essentially about Windows 98, the ECDL syllabus does not specify an operating system, so for most of the time in this book, we will use the Classic view, so that Windows 95 users (and there are still many) will find the information useful. There will, however, be occasions when we shall have to switch to the Web view to illustrate a particular point.

2.4. The Desktop

We have already seen the desktop in Figure 2.1. Note that it takes up the whole screen and, unlike any other window, you cannot make it smaller than the screen (except by adjusting the screen controls, but there is little point in that, unless you cannot see the whole desktop, because it simply reduces your working area). You may be able to make the desktop bigger than the screen, which can sometimes be useful, but we shall not consider that here.

You can also change the background, as we will see later in this section. When you first use your computer, it will probably be a single colour. On this background, you will see a number of icons. They may not appear exactly the same as Figure 2.1, because what appears depends on your system set-up, but there will be certain icons that nearly always appear. These include:

 My Computer: This is effectively the 'root' directory of the disks on the computer, as we shall see in the next section.

Network Neighborhood: This will only appear if your computer is linked to a network, for example in an office or college. Then it will always appear. It tells you about the other disk drives on the network that you can access.

My Documents: This is exactly what it says it is, a place My Documents where you can store your documents. While you can put them anywhere you like on the system, putting them here, usually in sub-directories with names that make sense to you, is a good idea. Apart from anything else, it makes backing them up much easier.

Internet Explorer: As already noted, the Microsoft Web Internet Explorer Browser comes with Windows 98 (but not with Windows 95). While there are advantages in using IE in the context of Windows 98, because they are closely integrated, some people prefer to use other browsers, such as Netscape Communicator or Opera.

Recycle Bin: This is important, because, by default, any file you delete from your hard disk is not actually deleted, but sent to the Recycle Bin, from where you can retrieve it if you find that deletion was not what you wanted to do. However, the Recycle Bin has a fixed size (although you can change it) and once it is full, the oldest files are automatically deleted to make room for the new. So, if you want to retrieve a file from the Bin, do not wait too long after you deleted it! Note that when you delete a file from a removable disk, you really delete it and you are unable to retrieve it.

My Briefcase: This is a folder that allows you to synchronise your files if you are working on more than one system, for example a desktop PC and a laptop. This is outside the ECDL syllabus.

Self Study

Click on each of the icons on your desktop to see what you find. Close them by using the X at the top right corner.

On the desktop, if you are using the Web view, you may also see the Channel bar, which is outside the scope of this book, although it may be referred to in Module 7, where the Internet is discussed. Then along the bottom of the screen is the Taskbar (Figure 2.7), made up of the following:

- **The Start button:** clicking this opens a quite complex menu (see below).
- **Running tasks:** these are the programs that are currently running or, to be strictly correct, the windows that are currently open, even if they are minimised, which means that the entry on the taskbar is the only visible evidence that they are running. The active window, i.e. the one you can see (or the one on top if you can see several), is highlighted. Clicking on any other activity will make that the active window. If the window is maximised, i.e. fills the full screen, then the new window will overlay the previously active window, while, if the window is not maximised, it will simply bring it to the front. Note that changing the active window does not affect anything that is happening in any of the windows.

Figure 2.7 The Taskbar located at the bottom of the screen.

Activities in different windows are effectively independent. Note that you can also switch between active windows by holding down the Alt key and striking the Tab key, as we shall see in Chapter 4.

● **Quick Launch toolbar:** this consists of the icons of programs you use frequently. You can launch (or open) these programs by clicking on the appropriate icon; mousing over them will open a box telling you what each one is.

● **The System Tray:** this contains the task scheduler, volume control and time and date, as well as icons representing various background tasks. These appear on the right-hand side.

Figure 2.8 Example of the Start menu.

The Start Menu is shown in Figure 2.8. Again, depending on how your system is set up, there may be various entries. Entries that will always be present, from the top of the second section down, are:

● **Programs:** selecting this displays the different programs and program groups. You can start programs from here, too.

● **Favorites:** selecting this displays Channels, Links and Software updates. We shall not look at this in any more detail in this guide as it is outside the ECDL syllabus. Nevertheless, if you are connected to the Internet, you will find it worth investigating.

● **Documents:** selecting this will display the last 15 documents you opened. They can have been opened in any application and a document here means any kind of data file, e.g. a word processing file, a graphics file, a spreadsheet, a database or a video clip.

● **Settings:** selecting this opens a menu including the Control Panel, Printers and even the Start Menu itself. We shall come back to some of these later.

● **Find:** selecting this opens a menu including Files and Folders. If you click this, you will open a window that allows you to specify searches on file and directory names. See Chapter 7.

● **Help:** selecting this opens up the Help facilities; we shall come back to this later in the chapter.

● **Run:** selecting this opens a dialogue box that allows you to start applications. This is effectively an alternative to using the Programs option at the top of the Start menu.

● **Log Off:** you may have no use for this, but it allows you to log off as one person or profile and then log on as another. This is outside the scope of the ECDL.

● **Shut Down:** clicking this allows you to close down or restart the system, as discussed above.

Self Study

Study the entries in the Start menu. See what happens when you select different options. You are unlikely to change your system unless you click **OK** after making any changes. So do not make any changes (unless you are confident), do not click OK; always click **Cancel**.

2.5. How to Look at Basic System Information

Exercise 2.5

You may want to know about your system, e.g. the operating system, the processor type, the amount of memory (Random Access Memory or RAM) installed. Most of this information you access via the **Control Panel**, which you open by clicking **Start** and then **Settings**. You will then see a window that looks like Figure 2.09. It may look rather confusing, but most of the icons are either self-explanatory or have complex names that probably mean that you will never have to be concerned with them. Here we want the one that (by default) looks like a computer and is labelled **System**. If you click that, you will open a window that looks like Figure 2.10. The first view is called General and tells you about your operating system, your processor type and who supplied it. This may be information that is useful when talking to dealers or support people.

Figure 2.9 The Control Panel.

Figure 2.10 The General view under System Properties.

There are three other tabs in this window:

● **Device information,** which describes the configuration of your system.
● **Hardware profiles,** which you are unlikely to need to access yourself. Incidentally, if you do access any of these out of interest and click on, for example, **Advanced Properties**, always click on **Cancel** rather than

OK, just to ensure that you have not inadvertently made any changes.

● **Performance,** which gives you more system information, such as the amount of RAM you have installed.

Self Study

Examine the System menu (remembering never to click **OK**).

2.6. How to Look at Basic Desktop Information

You may also want to look at information about the Desktop, including such things as screen settings, the time and date and other options, such as the (sound) volume settings. Again, you access the Control Panel. The following are some of the things you can view and change:

Exercise 2.6

● **Date and time:** Click **Date/Time**, which, not surprisingly, opens a window (Figure 2.11a) where you can set the date and time, as well as a second tab, where you change the time zone in which you live. You can also set the system to automatically correct the time for daylight saving (Figure 2.11b). Incidentally, when the clocks change, the computer informs you about it and asks you to check that everything is correct. If you just want to see the time, it is usually displayed in the bottom right corner of the screen. You will also find that mousing over the time will display the date. Note that to change the display format of date and time you need to go to Regional Settings (see below).

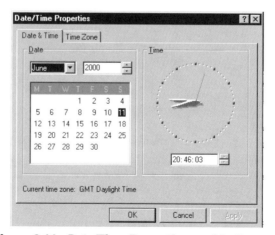

Figure 2.11a Date/Time Properties enable the user to set the date and time.

Figure 2.11b The Time Zone option under Date/Time Proerties.

● **Screen Settings:** click **Display** and then the **Settings** tab (Figure 2.12). Here you can see how the screen area (or resolution) and the colour scheme have been set. The screen area shows the number of pixels displayed, e.g. 800 x 600, and the colour scheme specifies how many colours are used on your Desktop (the more colours that are used, the more natural any photograph will appear). Details of these are outside the scope of ECDL, but changing the settings will illustrate what's involved. You can do no harm by changing the settings; you just reverse the operation to change them back. Note that the options you are given, and indeed how the screen will appear, will depend on your system (desktop or laptop, for example), on your screen size and on the software used to control the screen.

Figure 2.12 The Setting tab under Display Properties.

● **Colours and fonts:** click **Display** and select the **Appearance** tab.
Here you can choose the fonts and colours used on the Desktop (Figure
2.13). By selecting the different parts of the Desktop in the Item drop-down
menu, you can either specify a predefined scheme, such Brick, or you can
specify the colour (color) and font information (if the item includes text) in
the boxes shown. Once you are happy, you can just click **OK**, but it is
better to save your new scheme under a new name, so that you can come
back to it in future if you change schemes again.

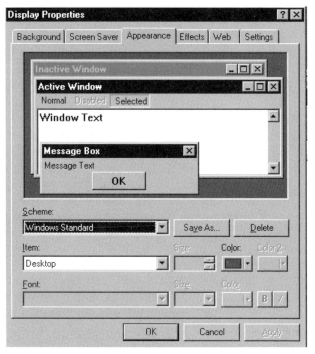

**Figure 2.13 Choosing fonts and colours using the
Appearance tab.**

● **Desktop Wallpaper:** this is the background to the icons on the Desktop
(it may have been called Wallpaper because it repeats). Click **Display** and
then the **Background** tab (Figure 2.14); you can also open this window
by right clicking on the Desktop background and then selecting
Properties. Changing the settings will illustrate the changes. Note that
you can either centre a pattern or picture, which is probably preferable if
you have a picture, or you can tile it, so that it repeats across the screen in
both directions. If you don't like what you see, then just change the settings
again; you can do no harm. If you do not like anything that Microsoft
provides, then you can use any graphics file or even a web page. To do

this click the **Browse** button and find the file you want to use. Click **Open** and you will see the file in the preview. If you want to use it then click **OK**. Windows 98 also allows you to choose Desktop Themes, but this is outside the ECDL syllabus (you may need your system CD in its drive if you want to investigate this option).

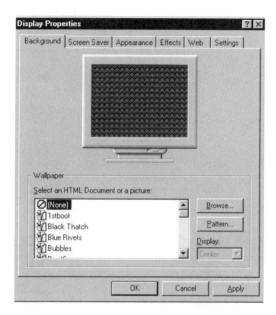

Figure 2.14 Selecting the Desktop Wallpaper using the Background tab.

● **Screen Savers:** Screen savers have two main purposes. The original one was to avoid the 'burn-in', an effect in which a picture displayed for too long became permanently etched on the screen. However, this is not really a problem with modern screens. The second reason is that they act as a security device, hiding what you are doing from prying eyes if you leave your desk. And, of course, they can be fun to look at. You choose them in a similar way to choosing a Wallpaper. Click **Display** and this time choose the **Screen Saver** tab. You will then see a window like Figure 2.15. You can then scroll through the available options, adjusting settings if there are any available and previewing if you wish. Note that you can also set a password and determine how long before the screen saver comes into effect. You will also see that there is a reference to power saving; this is when the screen goes completely blank in order to save electricity. Exactly how this is set up varies from system to system.

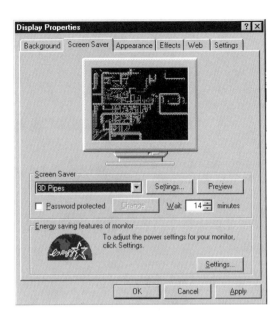

Figure 2.15 The screen saver options.

● **Regional settings:** clicking on this icon in the Control Panel opens a series of windows (Figure 2.16), within which you can view (and change) such things as the currency symbol in use, the character used for the decimal point, and the time and date formats. These are mainly self explanatory; the Time menu is not shown here.

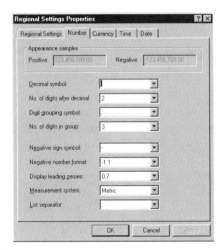

Figure 2.16a Specifying numbering settings.

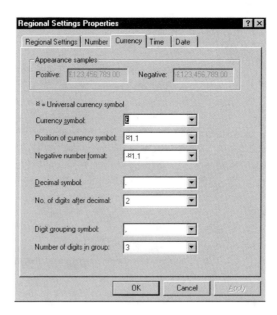

Figure 2.16b Specifying currency settings.

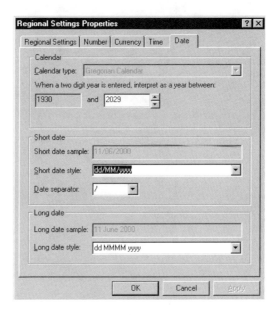

Figure 2.16c Specifying date settings.

● **Sound Volume:** The simplest way to control the volume is to use the volume control on the **Taskbar**. Just select it and you will see a slider control like those that appear on a hi-fi system. Move the slider to what is comfortable and then just click elsewhere to close the window. Note that there is also a **Mute** option, which can be useful in certain circumstances. If you do not see the symbol on the Taskbar, then click **Multimedia** and select the **Audio** tab, where, among other controls, you will see a slide bar labelled **Playback**. If you click this, you will open a window in which you can adjust the Volume control and the balance (Figure 2.17). (The other controls are outside the scope of ECDL.) When the volume and balance are as you want them, close this box by clicking the cross in the top right corner. In the main audio menu, you will also see a box that allows you to display the volume control on the Taskbar. If you select this option, then you will not need to open this, rather complex, Multimedia window again, unless, of course, you want to adjust the balance. To close the Multimedia window, click **OK**.

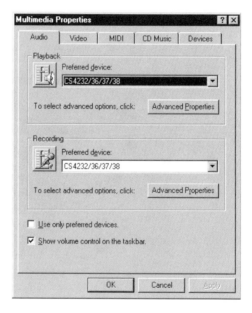

Figure 2.17 Adjusting the volume and balance.

Note that these are just some of the settings you can view and change via the Control Panel. You will learn about others if and when you need them.

Self Study

Look at the icons in the Control Panel and satisfy yourself that you understand what they are doing.

2.7. Finding Information about your Disks

To find information about your disks, the simplest way is to open **My Computer** and then select the disk you are interested in. You will then be able to see the size of the disk and how much free space there is on it. Exactly how this is displayed will depend on which Desktop view you are using; the Web view appears as Figure 2.18.

Figure 2.18 Checking information about your disks using Web view.

Self Study

Look at any other disks on your system, e.g. floppy disks, Zip drives or even network disks. You can try changing to the Classic view as well.

An alternative way to look at disk information is via Windows Explorer, which you can open by right clicking on **Start** and selecting **Explore**. When the window has opened, slide the scroll bar in the left-hand window to the top and you will then see a window like Figure 2.19. Select the disk you are interested in and select the **File** menu and the **Properties**. You will then see a window like Figure 2.20, which gives you the information you need.

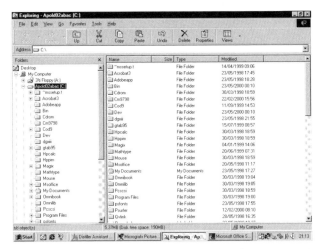

Figure 2.19 Looking at system details via Windows Explorer.

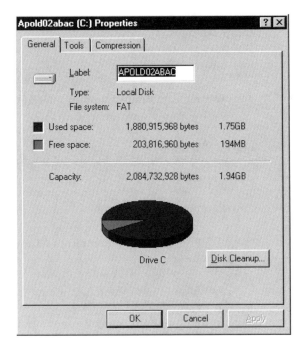

Figure 2.20 Obtaining disk information.

information

> **Windows Explorer: Windows Explorer allows you to look at your system in detail (Figure 2.19). The left window shows the hierarchical structure of the system. If a directory or folder has a small plus sign alongside it, this means that there are subdirectories that are currently not shown. Clicking on the plus sign will open up the structure and the sign will change to a minus. Clicking again on the minus will close the structure down. So, if you only want to look at the disks, you click on the minus signs within My Computer. The right-hand panel shows the directory that is currently open. You can open a directory by selecting it in the left-hand window. In the right-hand window, you can view the information in several different ways, as small or large icons, as a list, or with all the information about each file shown. If you select the View menu and look at the third section down, you will see these options. You will also note that you again see the options for arranging the icons. We will be looking at Windows Explorer in more detail in Chapter 5.**

2.8. Formatting a Diskette (Floppy Disk)

While you may never have to format a hard disk (and this is not covered within ECDL), you may frequently have to format a floppy disk. What this means is to organise the magnetic sectors on the disk surface so that they will store data in the format recognised by the Windows operating system, which organises the data differently from a Macintosh system, for example.

Exercise 2.8

To format a diskette, use the following steps:

step **1.** Open **My Computer** and select, but not open, the diskette drive – usually labelled 3.5-inch Floppy (A:).

step **2.** Open the **File** menu and select **Format**. This will open a window (Figure 2.21) with various options.

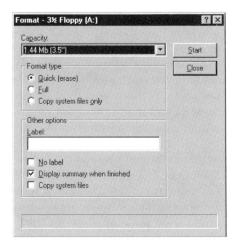

Figure 2.21 The floppy disk formatting dialogue.

3. Choose the type of disk and its capacity. Today, most 3.5-inch inch disks have a capacity of 1.44 Mb, but you may have a disk that has only 720 kb or even a 5.25-inch disk (these really are floppy!).

4. Choose the type of format. **Quick** can only be used if the disk has been previously formatted and really just erases any existing data. So for a new disk or one about which have little information, choose Full. The 'copy system files' options are only used if you want to create a diskette from which you can boot (start) your system. You may find that you need this if you have problems with your hard disk. Windows 98 prompts you to create such a 'boot disk' when you install it.

5. If you want to, give the diskette a label. You do not have to do this, but it can be useful. It is also a good idea to put a tick in the box alongside **Display summary when finished**. Sometimes diskettes are faulty and, if you see a summary, you can check that all has gone to plan.

6. Click **Start** and you will see a record of the progress being made and, if you have asked for one, a summary when the format is complete.

7. Finally, you will be asked if you want to format another disk.

Self Study

Take a used floppy disk and compare the time it takes to do a quick format and then a full format. Watch the progress and the messages.

2.9. How To Use Help Functions

Your system has extensive help built into it and you should get used to using this. These days, you do not get the large printed manuals that used to be provided and being able to use Help properly will make your life much easier.

Exercise 2.9

There are two ways of accessing Help:

● Go to **Start** and then select **Help**. This will take you in at the top level (see Figure 2.22).

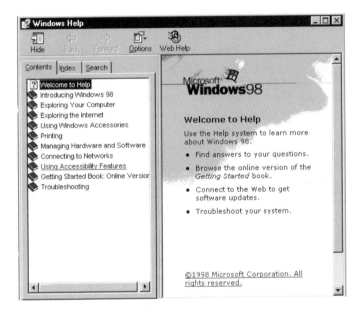

Figure 2.22 Accessing the Help functions.

● Press the function key **F1**. This will provide you with context-sensitive help, i.e. help about the part of Windows 98 that you are currently using, This will often be the better solution. See, for example, Figure 2.23.

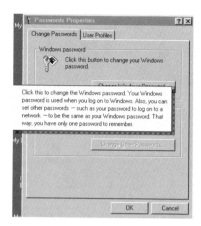

Figure 2.23 Example of context-sensitive help.

As you can see from Figure 2.22, Help is self-explanatory, as indeed it should be if it is going to be much use. A little explanation may be helpful, however, specifically of the tabs, **Contents**, **Index** and **Search**:

● Contents gives you the view shown in Figure 2.22. If you are learning about the system or are not really sure, this is probably the easiest approach.
● Index gives you a 'back-of-the-book' type index (see Figure 2.24). This is quick if you know what you are looking for and if you know the term Microsoft uses, which may not always be obvious!

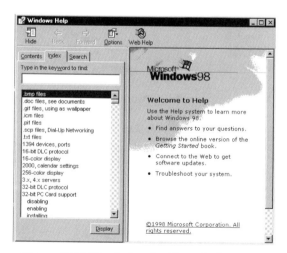

Figure 2.24 The Index facility within Help.

● **Search** (see Figure 2.25) allows you to search for any word. You put in the word or phrase and then click **Display topics**.

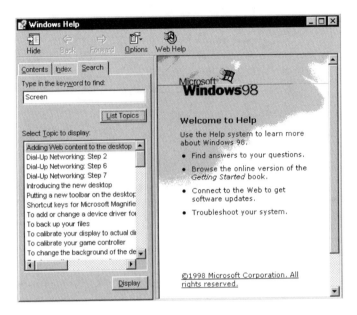

Figure 2.25 The Search facility within Help.

There are two other ways to get help:

● Right click on what you don't understand. If you see a box saying **What's this**, then clicking on it will give you an explanation. However, this may not always give you an answer that tells you what you want to know.
● In some windows (and most applications) there will be a question mark on one of the toolbars at the top of the window. Click on this and then click in the area where you are confused; an explanatory window will open. However, again it may not always tell you as much as you hoped for!

Self Study

Spend time using Help. Look through it first using the **Contents**. Then try looking in the **Index** or entering some search terms.

2.10. In Case of Difficulty...

Occasionally, for one of a number of reasons, an application will stop responding. This usually means that when you use the keyboard or click the mouse, nothing happens or perhaps whatever operation the system was carrying out just stops. You can usually tell because you can no longer hear the disk drive operating or the light that indicates that it is operating stops flashing. If this happens, try the following, in the order shown:

Exercise 2.10

1. Press the Esc (Escape) key on your keyboard. This may stop the operation in progress and let you give another command.

2. If pressing the Esc key has no effect, then hold down the Ctrl and Alt keys together and then press the Del (delete) key. This will bring up the Close Program menu. You will often find that the program you are using is at the top of the list you can see followed in brackets by 'Not responding'. In this case, click on **End Task**. This will close the program you are running. You will lose any changes you made since you last saved the file(s) you were working on. You may then just be able to start the application again. If another program shows 'Not responding', you can scroll down to that program and close that program. In such a case, because the result is unpredictable, it is a good idea to save your work and close the application you are running and restart the computer as described earlier. Indeed, you may find that even if it is the program you are running that has hit problems, they may recur, so restarting the computer is a good idea.

3. If you find that you cannot close the program, either because the Close program menu has no effect or because the cursor will not respond to the keyboard or the mouse, you can use Ctrl+Alt+Del again. This will restart your computer immediately without going through the Shut down procedure. (If Ctrl+Alt+Del has no effect, you can achieve the same result by pressing the reset button on your computer, if it has one, or in the last resort, switch the computer off and on again.) However, restarting your computer like this means that some system files may not be correct, so you will see a message that asks if you want to run a program, called ScanDisk, that checks your disk. To agree, you strike any key. Then follow the instructions you are given. ScanDisk will probably fix problems automatically, but if in any doubt, talk to an expert. (Note that ScanDisk may run without any intervention by you.)

4. Finally, there may be a serious problem with your system or your disk. While these are much rarer than they used to be, they do happen, particularly as systems get older. It is better to consult someone who knows about hardware. To try and maximise the benefits from their advice (for which you may have to pay), it is a good idea to have the boot diskette that Windows 98 prompts you to create on installation.

Summary

In this chapter:

- We have seen how to start, restart and shut down the PC.
- We have seen what to do if there are problems.
- We have examined the Windows desktop and learnt how to make adjustments using the Control Panel.
- We have seen how to obtain information about aspects of the system.
- We have seen how to format a floppy disk.
- We have looked at the Help system.

Working with Icons

In this chapter you will learn how to

- *Select and move icons.*
- *Recognise basic types of icon, such as directories and applications.*
- *Use shortcut icons.*

3.1. What are Icons?

If you have worked through the first two chapters, you will already have a good idea what icons are. Originally, icons were religious images, usually stylised, most commonly used in the Orthodox churches. However, in recent years, an icon has come to mean any image that represents an idea or an organisation. In computing terms, they are little pictures, which represent programs, files, directories etc.; within the Windows environment clicking or double-clicking an icon will trigger an operation of some kind. In order to help you, icons are generally designed to illustrate the operation they represent. After all, if they were all the same, they would not be much help. Indeed, in earlier versions of Windows, files, for example were all the same and you had to rely on the file name (usually shown below the icon) to identify the icon.

3.2. Selecting and Moving Icons

We have talked about selecting icons in Chapter 2. In Windows 95, to select, you just click an icon once and then to move it, you 'drag and drop'.

definition

> **Drag and drop: Drag and drop means that, instead of clicking on an icon, you place the cursor on the icon and depress the left mouse button. Keeping the button depressed, you move the cursor, dragging the icon with it, to the new position. Then you let go of the mouse button and the icon will stay in the new position if this is allowed; you may, however, get a warning message. You can also use drag and drop to move files between directories and even text in a word processing program.**

Exercise 3.2

In Windows 98, right click on the desktop and then select **Arrange icons**; see Figure 3.1. By default, icons are arranged in rows and columns. If you select **Auto Arrange**, you will remove the tick by it and turn off this automatic ordering. Then you can move the icons around using drag and drop or use the other options on the menu to arrange by Type, Size or Date. To tidy up the arrangement, just select **Line Up Icons**.

Figure 3.1 Selecting how to arrange icons.

3.3. Changing the Size of Icons and the Spacing Between Them

Auto Arrange usually gets the spacing between icons about right, but if you feel they are too close, then carry out the following procedure:

Exercise 3.3

1. Right click on the desktop and select **Properties**.

2. In the **Display Properties** dialogue box, select the **Appearance** tab (Figure 2.14 in Chapter 2). You can then select either the horizontal or the vertical icon spacing and adjust it; the default is 43 pixels.

3. When you have what you think is the right number, then click **Apply** to test it.

4. If it is correct, click **OK**.

Note that Auto Arrange must be ticked for Apply to show any proposed change.

To change the size of an icon, you go through a similar procedure:

1. Right click on the desktop and select **Properties**.

2. In the **Display Properties** dialogue box, select the **Appearance** tab. Then select **Icon** from the **Item** drop down list (see Figure 2.14 In Chapter 2).

3. In the **Size** box, change to a larger or smaller number; the default is 32 pixels.

4. When you have what you think is the right number, then click **Apply** to test it.

5. If it is correct, click **OK**.

If you change the sizes of the icons, the spacing will also change, so you may need to adjust that again. Note also that you are changing the size of all icons on your DeskTop.

Self Study

Experiment with changing the size and spacing of the icons on your desktop.

You can also change the size of the icons in your Start menu or on your TaskBar:

1. Click the Start button, and then select Settings.

2. Click Taskbar.

3. On the Taskbar Options (Figure 3.2a) or Start Menu Programs tab (Figure 3.2b), change the settings to what you want.

Figure 3.2a Changing icon size using Taskbar Properties.

Figure 3.2b Changing icon size using Start Menu Properties.

3.4. Changing Icons

You do not have to use the icons that have been provided for you. You can select others from amongst those stored on your system. The procedure is again similar:

Exercise 3.4

step **1.** Right click on the desktop and select **Properties**.

step **2.** In the **Display Properties** dialogue box, select the **Effects** tab (Figure 3.3, left).

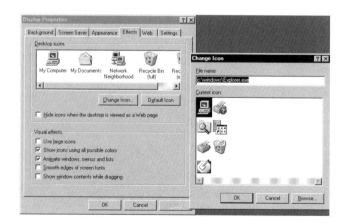

Figure 3.3 Selecting new icons from system options.

3. Select the icon you want to change at the top of the window and click the **Change Icon** button.

4. The **Change Icon** dialogue box will open and you can choose another icon (Figure 3.3, right).

5. If you are not happy with any of the choices provided, then you browse what is provided on the system, in either of the files Windows\system\shell32.dll or Windows\system\cool.dll (the latter may be what you are shown initially).

6. Select the icon you decide on and click **OK**.

Self Study

Try changing some icons. When you browse in the Windows\system directory, you can try opening any file that has an extension .dll (dynamic link library) or .exe (and executable file or program). Either of these file types may incorporate icons, although not all files do.

You can also download icons from the Web, but this is outside the scope of this book. Note that it is a good idea to be systematic about your icons; random selection can lead to confusion!

3.5. Basic Types of Icon

Some icons you will probably never change. For programs this is because the software suppliers have designed an icon for their program and changing it will only cause confusion. Similarly, there are some standard desktop icons, many of which we have already met. Typical ones are as follows:

 My Computer

 floppy disk

 network neighbourhood

 directory or folder

 recycle bin (waste basket)

When files are created by a particular application program, they will
have a file extension (the part of the file name after the full stop).
These extensions are automatically associated with a program (not
necessarily the one used to create them, so be careful) and the icon
representing a file will carry a modified version of the program icon.
For example, the Word icon is ✎, while the usual icon for a Word file
(with extension .doc) is ✎.

3.6. Creating a Desktop Shortcut Icon

Shortcuts are icons that you put, for example, on the DeskTop to give
you easier access to a particular program, folder or file, i.e. they are
pointers, also referred to as DeskTop aliases. You can recognise a
shortcut icon by the small arrow in the bottom left corner, thus ✎ is a
shortcut to Word, while ✎ is the real icon; the wording below the
icon may or may not say that the icon is a shortcut, so look for the
arrow. If you delete the shortcut, it is not important, because you can
always recreate it. However, if you delete the real icon, you will delete
the application, which is not usually what you want (while, as we have
noted in Chapter 2, you can recover files from the Recycle Bin, as long
as you realise in time that you have deleted them, it is better not to
have to use this option).

If you delete the file or folder to which the shortcut points, any
shortcuts to it are not deleted automatically. If you click on what might
be called 'orphan' shortcuts, you will see a message saying that
Windows is searching for the file to which the shortcut points, but that,
if you want to, you can use Browse to locate it yourself. This is
because, rather than deleting the file, you may just have moved it,
while the shortcut points to the original location.

Shortcuts can be created to any file, although usually they are to a
program or a folder. The Create Shortcut option appears in many
places, including:

● on the desktop pop-up menu (accessed with the right mouse
  button) as New/ShortCut;
● on various dropdown menus;
● on the pop-up menu you see if you right-click on an icon.

information

Keyboard shortcuts: Originally, shortcut meant a keyboard shortcut, but when Windows 95 was released, pointers, i.e. icon shortcuts, were introduced. So, when we say shortcut, we mean an icon. Keyboard shortcuts will always be referred to by the full term.

Exercise 3.6

There are various ways to create a shortcut; you will be realising by now that in Windows there is nearly always more than one way to do something. If you can see an icon, either on the desktop or in Windows Explorer (see Chapter 2), or even the file name in Windows Explorer, then do the following:

step **1.** Point to the object and right-click, keeping the button held down.

step **2.** Drag the object to the desktop; you will actually see an outline or ghost version of the object move, while the original stays where it was.

step **3.** Release the mouse button and you will see a menu like that shown in Figure 3.4a, although sometimes it will look like Figure 3.4b. This is because you are not allowed to move some icons, such as disk drives, as they form the structure of the filing system, as we shall see in more detail in Chapter 5.

Figure 3.4a Right-clicking and dragging an icon to the Desktop.

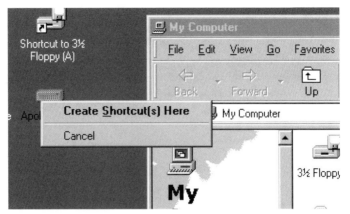

Figure 3.4b Releasing the right mouse button produces the menu shown here or that in Figure 3.4a.

Figure 3.4c Simply right-clicking (and not dragging) an icon produces this menu.

step**4.** Select **Create Shortcut(s) Here** and a shortcut icon will appear.

If you right click on the icon and do not hold the button down you will get a menu like Figure 3.4c. If you then select Create Shortcut, you will create a shortcut in the same folder as the real icon (if you are allowed to; sometimes you will get a message that you cannot do this and asking you if you want to create a shortcut on the desktop). Of course, a shortcut in the same folder as the real icon is not very useful, but once you have created it, you can always drag to the DeskTop or to a ToolBar. Alternatively, you can cut and paste the icon (see Chapter 6).

If you cannot currently see the icon you want, rather than using My Computer or Windows Explorer to locate it, you can do the following:

step**1.** Right-click on the Desktop.

step**2.** Select **New/Shortcut**.

step**3.** In the dialogue box that you will now see, type in the location and name of the original file (this is often referred to as the full path and will look like C:\Program Files\FrontPage Express\Bin\Fpxpress.exe). However, in many cases you will not remember what this is, so you can click the **Browse** button.

step**4.** Once Browse has opened a window that allows you to look around the system (Figure 3.5), find the file you want, select it and click **Open**. The Command line box will now show the path of the file.

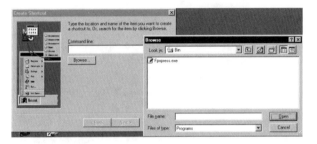

Figure 3.5a Creating a shortcut from the Desktop using Browse.

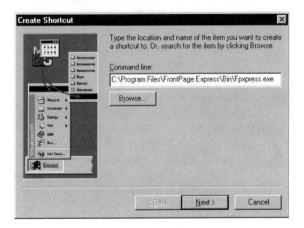

Figure 3.5b Creating a shortcut from the Desktop using the file location and name.

step**5.** Click **Next** and either accept the name given or put in your own; the system always gives a name that starts 'Shortcut to'.

step**6.** Click on **Finish** and the shortcut icon will appear on the desktop.

If you want to rename a shortcut (or, indeed, any icon), then just right click on it and select **Rename**. You then type in the new name and, to finish, click somewhere else or press the Enter key. Since Windows 95 there have been no practical limits on the names of files or icons, so it makes sense to use a description that you will understand. However, remember that the following characters are not allowed in icon or file names:

" * : | \ < > / ?

Self Study

Try creating some shortcuts on your desktop or in convenient folders. Try the different approaches outlined. Note that, as all you are creating are shortcuts, they may be deleted once you have finished.

information

The length of file names: On older systems, and perhaps networks that contain operating systems other than Windows 95 or 98, you may find that you are restricted to file names using what is called the 8.3 convention, that is eight characters before the full stop and three after. If you transfer files with longer names to such systems, then the names will probably be truncated and this can lead to confusion. It is also worth remembering that in Windows application files the file extension (the group of characters after the full stop) is associated with the application, so that changing a file extension from xls, for example, will mean that a file is no longer immediately identifiable as an Excel file, either by the system or by you. Of course, the file itself will not be changed, but a different extension makes it less easy to work with. And the whole point about many of the 'conventions' that have been introduced is that they are intended to make life easier for you. In general, once you get used to them, you will find that they do so.

You can change the properties of a shortcut by right clicking on the icon and selecting **Properties**. Then select the **Shortcut** tab. Most of these options are outside the ECDL syllabus, but a useful one may be the **Shortcut** key, which allows you to create a keyboard shortcut to, say, a program file. If you type in a letter, the system will add Ctrl+Alt. Thus, if you enter **F** for a program, then the keyboard combination to start the program will be Ctrl+Alt+F. As usual, you click **OK** to finish.

information

Keyboard shortcuts: It is a good idea only to have a few keyboard shortcuts, because these shortcuts take precedence over those used within application programs, where you will probably find that they are more useful, i.e. you save more time because you are carrying out an operation frequently. So, if you define a keyboard shortcut that is used in a program, then you will no longer be able to use the in-program shortcut.

There are various shortcuts that it is useful to create. For example, creating a shortcut on the DeskTop to a disk drive provides you with a much quicker way of seeing the contents than using Windows Explorer. Similarly, if you are on a network, you can add other computers to the DeskTop, or, if you access the Internet frequently, a shortcut to the Dialler will be useful.

Summary

In this chapter:

● We have examined how icons are used and how they can be created.
● We have also noted the difference between icon shortcuts and desktop shortcuts.

Working with Windows

In this chapter you will learn how to

- *Recognise the different parts of a desktop window.*
- *Reduce, enlarge, minimise and close a window.*
- *Recognise the aspects that all application windows generally have in common.*
- *Move between windows and between applications.*

Notice that we refer to windows with a small 'w', although of course these windows are an integral aspect of Windows 98.

4.1. Introduction

In Chapter 2, we spent some time looking at the main desktop window and much of what we said there is applicable to all windows. And we have already seen what windows look like; for example, clicking on **My Computer** opens a window that shows the disk-drive icons and various other directories and files.

4.2. What is a Window?

This may sound an unnecessary question to ask, but it is important to be clear. Windows are essentially of several kinds:

- those that represent a folder or directory, in which you can see the subfolders and files that are contained within that folder (the ECDL calls these desktop windows); we shall look at folders in more detail in Chapter 5;
- those that are menus or dialogue boxes; we have already seen some of these in previous chapters;
- application, or program, windows, which open when a program is started and represent the program environment; there may well be further windows that open within that window; these will be dealt with in other modules, although we shall briefly look at a simple text editor and a word processor in Chapter 8.

4.3. The Parts of a Desktop Window

Figure 4.1 shows a desktop window for the C: drive; this window has been chosen because there is more information than will easily fit in the window as shown. Figure 4.1(a) shows the Web view and (b) the Classic view. The main difference is that in the Web view the main area of the window is split, providing you with information in the left-hand pane; sometimes this is useful, but using the Classic view fits more files or information about them into the window. As we have noted previously, you can choose which you prefer and switch between them at will. We shall also see below that there are various different ways of displaying the information within the window. The options are the same for both views.

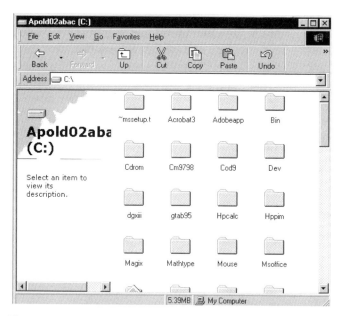

Figure 4.1a Desktop window for C: drive using Web view.

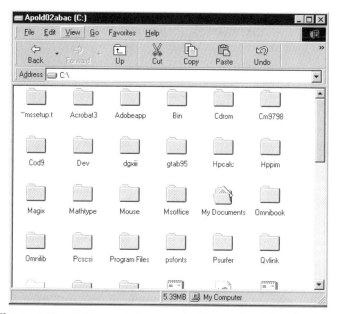

Figure 4.1b Desktop window for C: drive using Classic view.

At the top right of almost every desktop window are three icons. They are as follows:

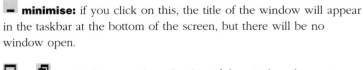
minimise: if you click on this, the title of the window will appear in the taskbar at the bottom of the screen, but there will be no window open.

☐ or ☐ **maximise** or **reduce in size**: if the window does not occupy the full screen, then you will see ☐, which means that the window will be maximised if you click on this; if the window is occupying the full screen, then you will see ☐ and clicking on this will reduce the window size.

✕ close: if you click on this, you will close (exit from) the application. If you click this in Word, depending on what you are doing, you may see a message on the screen, asking, for example, if you want to save the file you have been working on.

If a window does not fill the screen, it is a good idea to click on the centre icon of those above to maximise the window so that it fills the screen. Even then, you will see that the taskbar is still at the bottom of the screen.

The top line of the window tells you which window you have open. On the left there is an appropriate icon. If you click on that, the things you can do are self-explanatory. If you click **Move** or **Size**, then the cursor changes shape and allows you to move either the window as a whole or one of its edges. **Maximize** and **Minimize** have the same effect as the symbols at the top right of the window.

On the second line of the screen, there is also a list of words: **File**, **Edit** etc. These are menus and, if you select them, the menu will drop down. Depending on which view you are using you may just have to mouse over them (Web view) or click on them (Classic view). Move away (Web view) or click again or elsewhere in the window (Classic view) and the menu will close. Anything you can do with the window or the files within that folder can be accessed from these menus and we shall be looking at many aspects of them as we go through this guide.

Below the menus are one or more toolbars. Note that the toolbars contain icons that are graphical equivalents of the commands on the menus. Clicking an icon is often quicker than accessing the menu; what the icon does is usually printed below it in desktop menus; in application menus, you often have to mouse over to reveal the name of an icon. Some of these operations we shall discuss later, but a few are worth looking at now:

Back: this takes you to the last window you looked at. If the one on the screen is the first or only window you have looked at, then the icon will be 'greyed' out, which means that it is not operational.

Forward: this is often also 'greyed' out and will be when you open the window initially. However, if you move to another window and then back to the first, clicking on this icon will take you to the second window, and so on.

Up: this moves you up the directory structure, as we shall see in more detail in Chapter 5. So, if you are looking at the window for drive C:, clicking **Up** will move you to **My Computer**. You can see where you will move to by clicking on the down arrow at the right of the Address bar.

Undo: this is a very important operation (and applies everywhere in Windows). Click this and you will cancel the last operation you carried out (the keyboard shortcut is Ctrl+Z). Note, however, that this applies to editing operations, like Delete, and not to display options, in which you just choose another option. The difference is that display options, like changing a window size, only affect what you see. Editing operations actually change the files on your system!

Delete: If you select a file or folder within the window and then click this icon, you will see a message asking you either if you want to delete the file or if you want to transfer it to the Recycle Bin (with Yes and No options in each case). Which message you see will depend upon which folder you are looking at. If it is a folder on your hard disk, as we have discussed in Chapter 2, deletion just means copy to the Recycle Bin. However, if you are looking at a removable disk, then deletion means exactly that and the file is not recoverable – so be careful!

Properties: If you select a file within the window, then (usually, but not always) clicking on this icon will provide you with information about that file. The exact form of the information will vary depending on the type of file.

Views: Clicking on the down arrow to the right of this icon not only allows you to choose between the Web and Classic views, but also allows you to choose some other options (see Figure 4.2):

Figure 4.2 Options available under Views.

- large icons, as previously;
- small icons (Figure 4.3);
- a list (Figure 4.4);

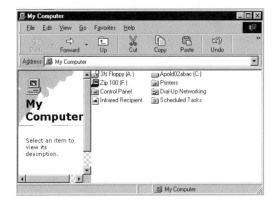

Figure 4.3 Selecting the small icons option.

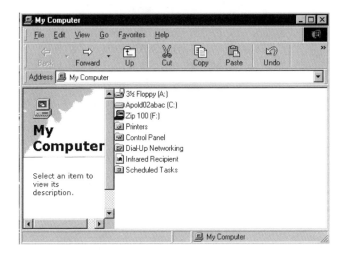

Figure 4.4 Viewing items as a list.

● a list plus details (Figure 4.5).

My Computer

File   Edit   View   Go   Favorites   Help

Back   Forward   Up   Cut   Copy   Paste   Undo   Delete

Address   My Computer

Name	Type	Total Size
3½ Floppy (A:)	3½ Inch Floppy Disk	
Apold02abac (C:)	Local Disk	1.94GB
Zip 100 (F:)	Removable Disk	
Printers	System Folder	
Control Panel	System Folder	
Dial-Up Networking	System Folder	
Infrared Recipient	System Folder	
Scheduled Tasks	System Folder	

My Computer

Select an item to view its description.

My Computer

Figure 4.5 Viewing items as a list plust details.

Remember that in the Classic view you see one pane and in the Web view two panes.

Self Study

Compare the different views of information in windows.

Below the toolbars is the Address window, which gives you the full address of what you are looking at. To move to another window, you can either type the new address in this window or, what is probably easier, browse by clicking the down-arrow at its right-hand side to display the structure of your system in a similar way to Windows Explorer.

Exercise 4.3

If the window contains more information than can actually be seen in the window, then on the right-hand side of each pane in the window is a vertical scroll bar which can be used to display the rest of the files. You can use this in several ways:

step **1.** Put the cursor on the sliding box and hold down the left mouse button. Then just move the mouse, and thus the box, up or down until you reach the line you want in the text.

step 2. Move the sliding box by pointing at either the single arrow at the top, to move up, or the single arrow at the bottom, to move down the document, and hold the left mouse button down until, again, you reach the line you want.

step 3. Click in the space above or below the sliding box and you will move up or down the document by one screen at a time; repeat until you reach the line you want.

There may also be a horizontal scroll bar at the bottom of the window. You can use this in the same way; just substitute left and right for up and down in the above descriptions.

There may be a third button or a scroll wheel on your mouse. Both are intended to make scrolling easier.

At the bottom of the window are three boxes, which may contain various pieces of information. These are:

Left-hand box: the number of objects in the window or the number of objects selected (if any are selected).

Centre box: the size of the file selected; if a disk is selected, the size of the disk and how much free space; if nothing is selected or if a directory is selected the box will be blank, as it will be if the directory only contains other (sub)-directories.

Right-hand box: where in the system you are, e.g. My Computer.

information

Note that, even when a window is set for full screen, you can still see the system taskbar at the bottom of the screen. Depending on how your system is set up, there may also be an Office toolbar (or maybe a Desktop or Accessories toolbar) down the right-hand side of the screen.

4.4. Moving and Resizing Windows

We have already looked at how you can resize a window using the icons in the top right corner of every window. You can also resize by placing the cursor on the edge of the window (if it does not occupy the full screen), and the cursor will turn into a double-headed arrow (Figure 4.6). You can then move in either of the directions indicated by the arrow to move that boundary of the window. If you place the cursor at a corner of the window, then you move both of the boundaries that meet at that corner. Selecting the icon in the top left hand corner and then choosing size allows you to do the same thing, but is an unnecessary stage.

Figure 4.6 The cursor turns into a double-headed arrow when resizing the window.

To move a window (providing it does not occupy the full screen), simply place the cursor on the title bar at the top of the window and drag and drop. Again, using the icon at the top left and the menu produced by selecting it allows you to do the same thing, but once more this is unnecessary. This menu also allows you to maximise, minimise and close the window (repeating the icons at the top right). Occasionally this may be useful because another window is obscuring your access to the top right of the window (some windows can be set so that they are always on top).

Self Study
Open some windows on the desktop and change their sizes by the various methods described above.

4.5. Applications Windows
Applications windows are similar to Desktop windows, except that they usually contain more toolbars, menus, etc. They are usually customisable and so may look different on different computers.

For standard applications, such as Word, Excel, Access and Internet Explorer, the windows will be explained in the appropriate module. Here we will look briefly at the Word window (Figure 4.7) so as to obtain a generic idea of the typical characteristics of an applications

★ ★ ★
★ ★
★ ECDL ★
★ ★
★ ★ ★

window. Most other applications will have a similar layout, but will vary in detail.

Exercise 4.5

Before we go on to describe the different areas of the screen, notice that, when Word starts up, it opens a new document, called Document1, for you; the name is given at the top of the window after the Word icon and, just to remind you, the words 'Microsoft Word'. In most cases you will not use Document1, but you can do so, typing in the text area and saving the document.

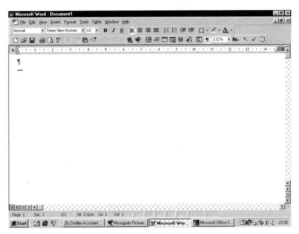

Figure 4.7 The Word window.

At the top right of the screen are three icons, common to all Windows applications and described above in Section 4.3.

The second line of the screen applies to the file you currently have open. On the left there is a **Word** file icon (a page with the Word icon superimposed). If you click on that, you will see a menu in which you can change the document window (which up to now is integrated with the Word window itself). If you click on **Restore**, the document window becomes separate (and the icon moves to that window). The other things in this menu we have already discussed.

On the second line of the screen, there are the menus, which are similar to those for the desktop windows. Anything you can do with Word can be accessed from these menus. See Module 3 for further details.

Below the menus are one or more toolbars. Note that the toolbars on your system may not be exactly the same as shown in Figure 4.7. Again the toolbars contain icons that are graphical equivalents of the commands on the menus; there are also a few icons at the bottom left of the screen. Clicking the icon is often quicker than accessing the menu; if you put your cursor on an icon (usually called mousing over it), the meaning of the icon will be displayed in a small box.

Self Study

Open Word and try mousing over the icons and opening the menus, so that you start to understand the window and its contents. (To open Word, the simplest approach is to go to **Start**, select **Programs** and then select **Microsoft Word**. To close Word, click on the **X** on the top right corner. If you are asked if you wish to save any files, then answer No.) Also open Excel in the same way and see the differences from, and similarities with, the Word window.

information

> **Toolbars do not have to be at the top of the screen; they can also be moved around the screen so that they float. If you want to use them in that way, you can, although most people leave them fixed at the top of the screen; the major benefit in doing this is that an icon is always in the same place.**

Below the toolbars is the ruler, immediately above the text window, which shows the margins you are using and any tabs you have set for the line you are on in the text. At the left there is a box showing the type of tab you can currently set. If you are in page view, there will also be a ruler down the left-hand side of the page. There will also probably be scroll bars on the right-hand side and at the bottom of the window; this depends on the whether the whole document or page can be seen within one window. Finally, within the Word window, you have a line, the status bar, that gives you more information such as the page and section showing on the screen, the total number of pages and whether, for example, you are in Insert or Overtype mode. For more information see Module 3 on word processing).

Applications obviously differ, because they are designed to fulfil different functions. However, virtually all applications have windows with a similar appearance to the Word layout, with menus and toolbars. What the menus and toolbars do will vary widely between applications, but generically they are the same. Similarly, scrollbars always work the same way.

4.6. Moving Between Windows and Between Applications

Windows is what is called a multitasking system, in that various different operations can be carried on at the same time. In fact, they all take turns to use the central processor, but this happens so fast that the user is not usually aware of it, at least in principle. Sometimes, however, mainly depending on what you are doing, how much memory (RAM) you have and how powerful or fast your processor is, the sharing is very obvious and you have to wait for a response from the computer. However, here we are only concerned with how you move between these applications that are running and between windows.

Moving between windows and applications is not quite the same thing, because, as we have seen, there are two kinds of window, desktop windows, which are almost literally windows onto part of the system, and application windows. Nevertheless, what you do is the same.

If you have a number of windows visible on the screen, i.e. none of them occupy the full screen, then the window that is active will have its title bar highlighted. Active means that any commands you type on the keyboard will apply to that particular window, and highlighted refers to the title bar which is a dark blue in Windows 98 as it is supplied (but this can be changed, so your system may be different). The title bars of all non-active windows will be 'greyed out'. If one window occupies the full screen (and you can see no other smaller windows), then this is the active window.

To make a different window active, you simply click in it if you can see it. While clicking anywhere in the window will have the effect of making the window active, it is safer to click in the title bar if you can. You then know that you cannot select a file or instigate a process inadvertently by holding down the mouse button for too long.

If you cannot see the title bar or if your active window occupies the full screen, there are two ways to move to another window. The first involves using the taskbar along the bottom of the screen, where all open windows are represented. To make another window active, just click the box on the task bar that represents it and the new window will open. This also applies if you have windows minimised, that is they only appear on the taskbar. If you are not sure which window is which, then just select until you have the one you want. Note that a full-screen (maximised) window will immediately occupy the full screen if selected, while any window that is not full screen will open on top of whatever was displayed before you made the selection (see Figure 4.8), unless you have a window set to be always on top.

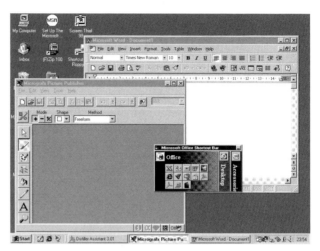

Figure 4.8 Example of windows opening on top of each other.

The final way of changing the active window is to use the key combination Alt+Tab. This opens a small window in the centre of your screen (see Figure 4.9) showing the open windows with the active window surrounded by a square and its title displayed below. If you hold down Alt and press Tab again, then you will see the square move to the next application and the title change appropriately. You can cycle through all the open windows. To make a window active, you simply release the keys when it is surrounded by the square. It is useful to note that, although you cycle through the operations, if you key Alt+Tab a second time, the previously active window will be active again. This can be very useful if you are switching backwards and forwards between two applications or windows.

Figure 4.9 Active window surrounded by a square.

You can, of course, also minimise the currently active window, but you will not usually be able to predict which window will then become active.

★ ECDL ★

information

You may wish to look at the desktop and minimise all windows. To do this right-click in a blank area of the Taskbar. Then you will see the menu shown in Figure 4.10a. Select Minimize All Windows. To restore all the windows to the state they were in before you minimised them, then right-click again in a blank area of the Taskbar Figure 4.10b and select Undo Minimize All. You will see that the menu you opened by right-clicking the taskbar also shows other options. We will not deal with Toolbars here, but the effects of the three options for arranging windows are shown in Figures 4.11 to 4.13.

Figure 4.10a Menu option to Minimize All windows.

Figure 4.10b Menu option to restore all windows to their state before the Minimize All command was applied.

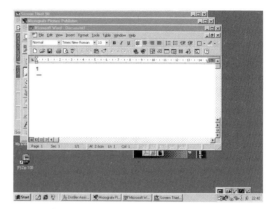

Figure 4.11 Example of Cascading windows.

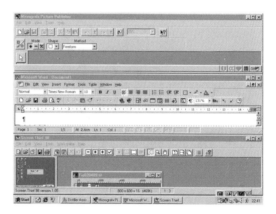

Figure 4.12 Example of windows Tiled Horizontally.

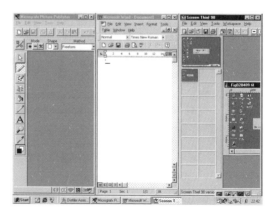

Figure 4.13 Example of windows Tiled Vertically.

information

Whenever you change the active window, it is a good idea to save the file you are working on in the currently active window. While, in principle, you should be able to go back and save it, things do sometimes go wrong and, even though Windows does have ways of getting back files that have been lost or corrupted, they are not foolproof and anyway it is better not to need them!

Summary

In this chapter:

- We have looked at what windows are.
- We have looked at the parts of a desktop window.
- We have seen how to move and resize windows.
- We have looked at the parts of an application window.
- We have seen how to move between windows and applications.

File
and Directory
Structures

In this chapter you will learn how to

- *Utilise file and directory structures.*
- *Create directories and subdirectories.*
- *View the properties of a directory.*
- *Recognise different types of icons representing files and how to view the properties of these files.*
- *Rename files and directories.*

5.1. Directory Structures

Some of these topics we have touched on before, but here we will attempt a systematic approach.

To look at directory (or folder) structures we really need to understand the overall structure of the file system, which we mentioned in Chapter 1, where we talked about filing cabinets and inverted trees. The concept is very simple; you can either think of files as folders within other folders within filing cabinet drawers within the cabinet, within the filing room etc.; alternatively you can think of them as leaves growing on twigs, growing on branches, growing on bigger branches, growing from the root (for some reasons the trunk never features, but this may be because the terminology originated in the USA and the trunk means what we in the UK call the car boot!). Figures 5.1 and 5.2 repeat the figures from Chapter 1 that we used to illustrate these concepts. Remember that, from a practical viewpoint, there is no limit to the number of levels of sub-directories you can create, although you will find that, unless you are systematic and use a structured approach, creating too many levels will mean that it is difficult to remember where files are.

Figure 5.1 Windows uses cabinet and folder metaphors for the file structure.

Figure 5.2 The inverted tree metaphor can be used for the file structure.

Self Study

Look back at the work you did in Chapter 1 and see if you feel that the directory structure you designed there for your ECDL work is still appropriate or does it need modifying?

shortcut

> **Although when you look at your system, you see an organised structure, in fact the files are not stored like that at all. They are scattered in small sections all over your hard disk and the operating system handles the task of linking all those pieces together and relating them to the file names you (and Microsoft and other vendors) have given them. In fact, after some time the pieces can become so scattered (the files are described as fragmented) that access to them slows down. Windows provides what is called a defragmentation tool to sort out this situation. If you think that this may be a problem, talk to someone with experience about it.**

We have already seen how opening a window representing a folder shows you the files and other folders within that folder. We shall look again at this when we look at information about files (Section 5.6).

5.2. The Structure of Files

In fact, we are not really going to discuss the structure of files, or least their internal structure, because that is determined by the application that was used to create the file. We shall look at simple text files in Section 5.8, but other file structures are not readable without the application that created them (or a compatible application). Such structures include not only what you see on the screen when you open an application, but many other codes that tell the application what to do with the data you see.

5.3. How To Create Directories and Sub-Directories

There are two usual ways to create directories and sub-directories, by using Desktop windows and by using Windows Explorer.

★ ECDL ★

Exercise 5.3

From the Desktop, you do the following:

step 1. Open **My Computer** and select and open folders until you reach the folder where you want to create a new (sub)folder. Of course, if you already have a short cut on your desktop to this folder, you can open it directly. Alternatively, you can type the full path name in the Address box.

step 2. Open the **File** menu and select **New**. Another menu will appear to the right, with **Folder** and **Shortcut** at the top (Figure 5.3). (We have already seen this in Chapter 3.)

Figure 5.3 Menu for creating new folder.

step 3. This time select **Folder**. A new folder will appear in the window (after the existing files, irrespective of alphabetical order), labelled, not surprisingly, New Folder; these words will be highlighted (Figure 5.4). This will be true whatever view of the information you have chosen.

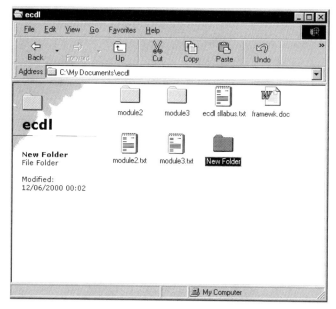

Figure 5.4 Creation of a new folder.

step **4.** Type the name you want to give the folder and then strike the Enter (Return) key or click somewhere else. The folder will have the name you have given it. If you do not give it a new name, perhaps clicking somewhere else inadvertently, which is particularly easy to do in the Web view, then you can rename it, as described in Section 5.7. Next time you open this folder window, the file will be in the correct place, depending on how you have decided to view the files, by date, name, etc.

From Windows Explorer the stages are very similar:

step **1.** Open **Windows Explorer**.

step **2.** Select the directory or folder within which you wish to create a new folder.

step **3.** Open the **File** menu and select **New**.

After this the stages are the same again. The new folder will appear in the pane of the Explorer that shows the Directory content. Again it depends how you are displaying the file names on exactly what will appear. Figure 5.5 shows the folder window, with Large Icons selected. Figure 5.6 shows Windows Explorer with Details selected.

Figure 5.5 Folder window with Large Icons selected.

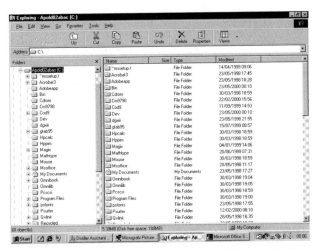

Figure 5.6 Folder window with Details selected.

As noted above, there is no practical limitation on the number of levels you can nest directories or folders, so to create a folder within your new folder, you simply open the new folder and repeat the process.

Self Study

Create the ECDL file system that you reviewed in Section 1 of this chapter. My Documents is a good place to put it.

5.4. Examining a Directory/Folder

So you have opened the window representing a directory or folder. What else can this tell you? Similarly to the way we looked at information about disk drives in Chapter 2, we can look at files or directories in folders other than via **My Computer**. So to get information about a directory, you look not in its own window, but in the window of its parent directory, where if you select the icon for the child directory, you will see, in the Web view only, information about the child directory in the left pane (see Figure 5.7). For a file, you can see similar information (Figure 5.8). In the Classic view, this information is not displayed. For a file you can obtain the same information and more by accessing the properties (by using the icon on the toolbar, selecting **Properties** in the **File** menu or selecting **Properties** from the menu produced by right clicking) – see Figure 5.9. However, if you do this for a directory, you see the date it was created, rather than the date it was modified. This may seem rather inconsistent – and indeed it is, but it is so easy to switch between views that one can regard this as a richness rather than an oddity.

Figure 5.7 Accessing directory information in Web view.

Figure 5.8 Accessing file information in Web view.

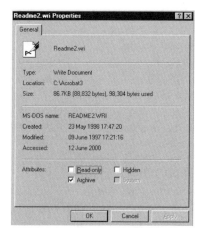

Figure 5.9 Accessing file information from Properties in Classic view.

As we have seen, the name of a directory or a file is displayed below its icon in the parent directory window and, of course, it is displayed in the title bar of its own window.

If you use the Details view, you will be able to see much of the same information about the files and directories, but in a more compact form (as in Figure 5.10). Note that you can always obtain the same information in the same format via Windows Explorer, so the option you take will depend on what you find simpler. We shall look at file attributes below.

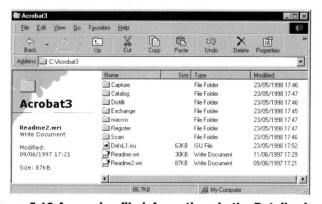

Figure 5.10 Accessing file information via the Details view.

If you open the directory or folder of interest, as we saw in Chapter 4, the first two boxes at the bottom of the window give you information about the number of files in the directory and the size of the file selected. In Windows Explorer, however, the middle box shows the combined size of all the files in the directory (if none of the files are selected).

Self Study

Select a file and a directory and see what you can find out about them, using the approaches given above.

5.5. Common Types of File

You will have noticed that files have different icons associated with them. While these can be chosen at random, in fact they represent the application that is associated with that type of file. This may be the program used to create the file, but not necessarily, and there is occasionally confusion, because the association is based on the file extension (the letters – usually three – after the dot in the file name) and sometimes you find that two applications use the same extension. On the whole, though, this is not common and certainly not so for the most frequently used files.

Figure 5.11 Shows a window containing a number of application files. You will see, as we noted with the Word window in the previous section, that the icon usually contains the application icon. Common file extensions and icons include the following:

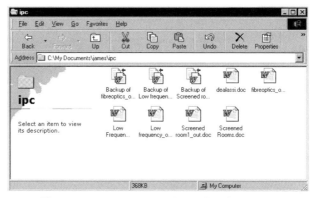

Figure 5.11 A number of application files.

.exe. This is an executable file, i.e. a program. Programs tend to have the icon of their application, as we have seen for Word.

.bat. This is another type of program file.

.com. This is yet another type of program file (for the purposes of ECDL you do not need to understand the differences between the types of program file).

 .doc. This is usually a Microsoft Word file. However the icon can also represent an RTF file, which is also usually a word processing file, in Rich Text Format, which will be considered in more detail in Module 3. RTF files are in a form such that the formatting commands can be read as text. This format is often used as an exchange format between word processing programs and as a safe way of sending a word processing file via email, if viruses are likely to be a problem.

 .txt (or sometimes .asc). This is usually a plain text file. The .asc is short for ASCII, which is the name of the coding system used for the alphabet, numerals and a few other symbols.

.xls. This is almost always an Excel spreadsheet file.

.ppt. This is usually a presentation file produced using Microsoft PowerPoint.

.pdf. This is almost always a file in Portable Document Format (produced and read with Adobe Acrobat software). It is effectively an electronic facsimile of a printed page, which can be read using the freely available Acrobat reader.

.zip. This is a compressed file format, which is frequently used to transfer large files either on disk or across the Internet.

 .htm. This will be an HTML (hypertext) file that represents a World Wide Web document. Note that the icon given here is that of Microsoft's web browser, called Internet Explorer. There are other browsers, the most common of which is Netscape Navigator. If your system is set up to use this, rather than Internet Explorer, then you will see the Navigator icon.

.jpg. This is an image file in JPEG format. This format, named after the Joint Photographic Experts Group, is widely used on the web. The icon used here is for Micrografx Picture Publisher, but there are a large number of different picture editing files available, so your system may show a different icon.

Exercise 5.5

This is just a sample list of common file types. If you go to either My Computer or Windows Explorer and open **View** and then **Folder Options**, you will open first the window in which you can choose the view that you want to use. However, if you click on the **File Types** tab, you will see a window that looks like Figure 5.12, which indicates what each of the icons represents. If you select one, in the area below you will then see the icon, the file extension and the program that opens this file by default, i.e. if you open it in a window or in Windows Explorer. As you will see in Figure 5.12, you can change these, remove them and add new ones, but that is outside the ECDL syllabus.

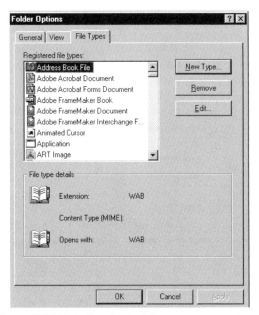

Figure 5.12 Details of what icons represent can be found in File Types.

If a file has the generic Windows icon (⬛) associated with it, this means that Windows does not recognise the icon and therefore, when you open the file by clicking on it, a window will open (rather like Figure 5.13) in which you are asked to select the application program that you wish to use to open the file.

Figure 5.13 Icons can be changed, removed or added.

5.6. File Attributes

We have already talked about file properties – otherwise known as attributes. If you use the Details option to look at a window or within Windows Explorer, you will see these. A detailed view is shown in Figure 5.14. The attributes are:

Name	Size	Type	Modified
graphics		File Folder	11/06/2000 17:39
Backup of Figcaps...	24KB	Microsoft Word Bac...	12/06/2000 17:44
Backup of section...	29KB	Microsoft Word Bac...	12/06/2000 13:27
Backup of section...	62KB	Microsoft Word Bac...	12/06/2000 14:50

Figure 5.14 Examples of file attributes.

File name: This is not as absolute as you might think, because you can change the name of a file, as we shall see in the section below, without changing the contents and nature of the file at all. However, if you try to change the extension (and by implication the file type), then Windows will ask you if you mean to do this. As we have discussed, the name is preceded by an icon.

File size: This is given in bytes, where effectively a byte represents a character or a code. Thus, although a text file may contain 400 words with perhaps 2,500 characters (including spaces and carriage returns), a formatted Word file of the same text may have a size that is ten times as great because of the inclusion of the formatting information. You need to keep an eye on file sizes, because eventually you may run out of disk space, although disks are now so large that this becomes increasingly unlikely. Size can also be important, however, if you are transferring a file, either on disk or over the Internet.

Type: This is almost redundant, but it confirms what the icon shows you about the file.

Modified: This shows the date and time that the file was either created or last modified. If this is a file that you have created, then it is straightforward. However, sometimes files that have come from elsewhere may show the date and time that they were transferred onto your system or even some other date. So do not put too much trust in this information, except for your own files, which are likely to be the ones where this information is most important. If the date and time are shown in a format that you do not like, then you can change it, as we discussed in Chapter 2 (using International Settings – not Date/Time – in the Control Panel).

Self Study

Examine the attributes of different kinds of files. Are some types of files smaller than others? Are the system files older. Find some files that have never been modified. In all, try to understand what the file attributes can tell you.

5.7. Renaming Files and Directories

We have mentioned renaming when discussing the creation of a new file and we have already discussed renaming short cuts. The procedure for renaming files and directories is very similar:

Exercise 5.7

step 1. Select the file or folder that you want to rename, either in My Computer or Windows Explorer.

step 2. Choose Rename from the File menu or from the menu produced by right clicking. The existing name will be highlighted.

step 3. Type the new name and either click elsewhere or strike the Enter/Return key.

Next time you open the window or change the order to alphabetical, the file will appear correctly under its new name. As noted above, if you try to change a file extension, Windows will ask you if you really want to do this.

Self Study

Experiment with renaming files. See what happens when you try to rename a program file. (It is probably better to follow the advice given.)

Summary

In this chapter:

- We have looked at directory structures.
- We have realised that we can only look at the external structure of files.
- We have learned how to create directories and sub-directories.
- We have looked at how we can obtain information about directories and files.
- We have looked at common types of file.
- We have considered file attributes.
- We have seen how to rename files and directories.

Selecting, Copying, Moving and Deleting Files and Directories

6

In this chapter you will learn how to

- Select files.
- Copy and move files and directories.
- Delete files and directories.
- Copy files to a diskette as backup.

6.1. Introduction

This chapter is about doing what one might call secretarial or administrative things with files and directories as entities. In other words, think of a file in conventional terms, that is as a bundle of papers, which you can choose from the filing cabinet, move around, throw away and even copy without actually referring to the contents of that file. Just as you can do these things with a real file of papers, so you can do them, rather more easily and certainly with less effort, with files and directories on your computer. Copying the complete contents of a directory can be achieved with a few clicks of the mouse button.

To save repeating the phrase 'file or directory', throughout this section when we say file this means either a file or a directory.

6.2. Selecting Files

If you want to carry out an action on a file, the first thing you need to do, as we have already seen in previous sections, is to select it. You have already seen how this is done and you know that, if you are in the Web view, you only have to move the cursor over the icon or file name representing the file, while in the Classic view you click once on the icon or file name. It is obviously easier just to have to move the cursor to the file, but in the Web view if you move the cursor onto another icon, then that icon is selected instead. On the other hand in the Classic view the file you have selected remains selected until you make a decision to select another file, or de-select the first one by clicking it again or clicking in a blank area of the window (with the Web view, just moving the cursor to a blank area deselects the file).

Exercise 6.2

Before we go on to consider what you can do once you have selected a file, we shall look at ways in which you can select more than one file:

● To select all the files in the active window, open the **Edit** menu and choose **Select All**. Even easier is to use the keyboard shortcut and enter Ctrl+A.
● To select adjacent files, you can select one and then hold down the Shift key as you select others. All those you passed your cursor over in the Web view or clicked on in the Classic view will then be included in the selection. If you are looking at icons you can also marquee select. This means that you draw a box in the window by clicking at an appropriate blank spot in the window and hold down the left mouse button until the box includes all the files you want to select; then you release the mouse button and those files will be selected. See Figure 6.1.

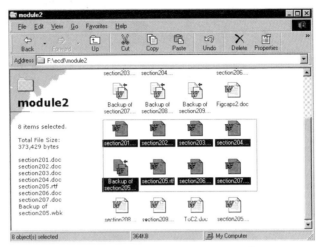

Figure 6.1 Using the marquee select feature.

● To select non-adjacent files, you again select the first one you want and then hold down the Ctrl key while you either click on the others you want in turn (Classic view) or pass the cursor over them (Web view). The latter is more difficult because you have to take what may be a rather complex path with the cursor in order to avoid all the files you do not want to select. Here, using the Classic view certainly seems simpler.

To de-select a particular file you effectively repeat the process on the files that have been selected. Thus, if you want to de-select a series of adjacent files (and they have to be at the beginning or the end of the selection), de-select the first or last and, keeping the Shift key depressed, click in the Classic view or move the cursor over the file in the Web view for each of the other files you want to de-select.

In fact, it is generally easier to hold down the Ctrl key and de-select files one by one (and here they do not have to be at the beginning or end of the selected list).

Self Study

Experiment with different methods of selecting and de-selecting files to see which you prefer.

6.3. Copying and Moving Files

We have already seen that you can move icons by using drag and drop. That is, you select a file and then, holding down the mouse button, you drag the icon (or file name – it works with file names as well) until it is where you want it, when you release the mouse button. In fact, you can carry out drag and drop in more than one way. If you use the left mouse button, as we have done previously, then, if the target window is on the same disk drive (i.e. it has the same letter such as C:), the file will be moved. However, if the disk drive has a different letter (e.g. a diskette A:), then a copy will take place. The reason for this is obvious; it reduces the risk of files being lost. While you have the button held down, if a copy is due to take place, a small plus sign appears. If the file is a program file (with a .exe or .com extension), instead of the plus sign you will see the Shortcut arrow appear, because instead of either a copy or move, a shortcut will be created. This is because moving program files can mean that they will not operate properly. In fact, if you open the Program Files window, you will see a warning to this effect in the Web view. The different versions of the icon as it is moved are shown in Figure 6.2.

Figure 6.2a The '+' symbol indicates an icon is being copied.

Figure 6.2b No '+' symbol means the icon is being moved.

An alternative approach is to use the right mouse button when you drag and drop. This time (whatever the target window), when you release the mouse button, you will be given four options, Move Here, Copy Here, Create Shortcut(s) Here and Cancel. This is probably the easiest and least risky approach, other than using the Clipboard, which we shall describe in Section 6.4.

Selecting and moving or copying groups of files is not always as simple as it sounds, because, unless you are careful, you can find that you have changed your selection without intending to do so, just because your timing was not quite right. So, if you plan to use this approach, it is a good idea to practise.

In addition, drag and drop really requires you to have both the source area or window and your target area or window visible on the screen at the same time. While you can drag and drop off the screen by moving the cursor to the edge of the screen, what happens then is not always easy to control.

Thus, an alternative method is useful. This uses what is called the Clipboard and techniques called Copy, Cut and Paste.

6.4. The Clipboard, Copy, Cut and Paste

Exercise 6.4

To copy a file or group of files from one directory to another, you first select what you want to copy and then choose **Copy**, either from the **Edit** menu of the window where you are viewing the file(s) (this can be either My Computer or Windows Explorer) or from the pop-up menu you see when you right click on your selection. What happens then, although this is not obvious from what you see on the screen (nothing appears to happen), is that the files you have selected are stored (usually described as placed) on the Clipboard, which you can think of as a special area in the computer memory. The term Clipboard is used because, if you think of the physical analogy, you can take a piece of paper and add it to a clipboard until you decide where it should be re-filed.

If you decide that, instead of copying a file, you want to move it, then instead of choosing Copy from the **Edit** menu or the pop-up menu, you choose **Cut**. This time you will see something happen; the selected file(s) will change in appearance, becoming faded with the outlines dotted (see Figure 6.3). Again the file has been copied to the Clipboard.

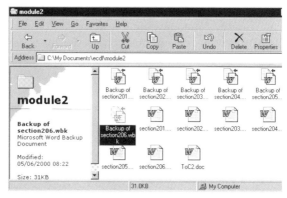

Figure 6.3 Result of selecting Cut from the Edit menu.

In either case, you then open your target window (again either in My Computer or in Windows Explorer) and go again to the **Edit** menu or the pop-up menu produced by right clicking and select **Paste**. The file (or its icon) will then appear in the new window. You will also notice that, if you **Cut** the original file, it will now disappear from the original window.

shortcut

Note that when you use the Clipboard, it does not matter whether the target window is on the same disk or not; the operation is the same. The other thing to note is that the Clipboard will retain a file name (and in fact other types of data, e.g. text from a word processing program) until either you turn your computer off or you carry out another Cut or Copy operation. Thus, you can Paste the contents of the Clipboard in more than one place (this is more useful with text than with files), but remember that if you do Cut or Copy something else, then what was previously on the Clipboard is lost (although you can use Undo – Ctrl+z). Of course, if you copied, then this is not a problem. However, if you are cutting, then you need to be careful; that is why the faded image is shown until you have pasted. It is possible to obtain programs that allow more than one item to be retained on the Clipboard and, indeed, Windows 2000 allows a few items to be retained.

The keyboard shortcuts for Copy, Cut and Paste are probably some of the most widely used. They are:

● Copy: Ctrl+C
● Cut: Ctrl+X
● Paste: Ctrl+V

You will note that, along with Ctrl+Z (Undo), they are at the bottom left of the keyboard and, even for one-finger typists, are easy to access.

The other point worth noting is that all the move and copy operations can be reversed with Undo (Ctrl+Z).

6.5. Deleting Files and Directories

Exercise 6.5

Deleting files is similar to copying and moving, except that once you have selected the file(s) you want to remove, you either click the right mouse button or you go to the **File** menu of the window containing the file(s) you want to delete and select **Delete**. Even simpler is just to depress the Del (delete) key on your keyboard. Whichever of these three options you take, you will then see a message asking you to confirm the deletion (Figure 6.4). In fact, the message will be different depending on where the file is situated. As we have noted in Chapter 3, files deleted from the hard disk are actually moved to the Recycle Bin so that you can get them back again, while files deleted from a floppy disk are actually deleted (even Undo does not work here). So you need to be sure that you do indeed want to delete these files.

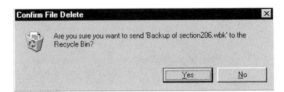

Figure 6.4a Files deleted from the hard disk are sent to the Recycle Bin.

Figure 6.4b Files deleted from floppy disks are erased immediately.

If you indicate that you want to delete a directory, the message you see will ask if you want to delete/move to the Recycle Bin the directory and all its contents, just to remind you that this is not just a single file that you want to remove. You can also drag and drop a file to the Recycle Bin window (or onto its icon), but, if you do that, you will not see the message asking you confirm the operation.

If when you use a menu to delete, you hold down the Shift key when you select **Delete**, then, irrespective of which disk the file is situated on, you will delete rather than copy to the Recycle Bin. This may be useful if you have a confidential file that you want to remove, but again be very sure that you do want to remove it completely.

★ ECDL ★

6.6. Copying Files to a Diskette as Backup

While good practice is strictly not part of this ECDL module, we should stress that it is important to remember to back up your work, i.e. copy to a removable medium, just in case something goes wrong with your computer system or perhaps you delete a file inadvertently. These removable media include diskettes, tapes, removable disks such as Zip disks, and even recordable or rewritable CDs. Although it is most important to copy your work regularly, a complete system backup is also useful at regular, if longer, intervals.

Although special software is obtainable for handling backups, you can simply copy the files from your working window (probably within the My Documents directory) to the window that represents the diskette (usually your A: drive) or whichever medium you wish to use for backup. Indeed, all you need to do is select the files or directories that you want to back up and drag and drop them to the new window, remembering that, because this is a different disk, the result will automatically be a copy rather than a move.

If you are moving files to a disk that already contains files or directories with the same names, then you will receive a message asking if you want to replace the files or directories with the new ones. This message even gives you the dates on which the two files of the same name were last updated (see Figure 6.5), so all you have to do is click Yes or No. There is also a button that allows you to indicate Yes to All, which saves you having to look at every file individually, but to use this you need to be sure that you do want to replace the old files with the new ones. For backup purposes this usually is the case.

Figure 6.5 Message requesting confirmation of file replacement.

Summary

In this chapter:

- We have seen how to select files and groups of adjacent and non-adjacent files.
- We have seen how to copy and move files with the mouse.
- We have seen how to copy and move files by using Copy, Cut, Paste and the Clipboard.
- We have seen how to delete files and directories.
- We have seen how to copy files to a diskette or other removable media for backup.

Searching for Files and Directories

- *Use the Find tool to locate a file or directory.*
- *Use different properties of a file to locate it.*

7.1. Introduction

Although it is important to organise your directory structure so that you know where different files are, even in the best regulated systems there comes a time when you want a file and you cannot be sure where on the system it is. And the larger hard disks become and the more space software takes up, the more likely this is to happen.

Fortunately, Windows provides you with an important tool called Find to look for files and directories, while there are other tools, which we will not discuss here, but which will be referred to in Module 7, for finding information on the World Wide Web.

7.2. Using Find

Exercise 7.2

To open **Find**, click on **Start**, select **Find** and then **Files and Folders**. The window shown in Figure 7.1 will open. By now you should find this fairly self-explanatory.

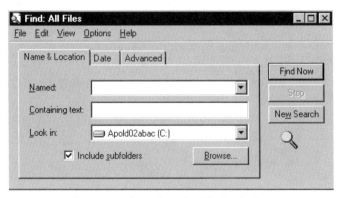

Figure 7.1 Opening the Find window.

The first tab you see is the Name & Location tab. There are two main ways in which you can search, either by the name of the file you are looking for or by a string of text that occurs within the file you are looking for. You can also combine the two. We shall look at this tab first. Then we shall look at the other tabs, Date and Advanced, as well at one or two of the menu options.

7.3. A Simple Search

We shall start with looking for a file that is on every Windows system, one called config.sys. This is a file that is invoked when Windows starts up.

Exercise 7.3

To find where it is on the system, you simply type *config.sys* into the **Named** box. You also need to tell the system where to look by completing the **Look in** box. By default you are usually given the name or code for your hard disk (C:), but you can browse your system in the usual way to make the search more specific and, incidentally, reduce the search time. On the other hand, you increase the scope of your search if you include removable disks, such as CDs, and other computers on the network.

It is usually a good idea to have the box **Include subfolders** ticked. If you do not, then the search will only look for files within the top-level directory. So, if you have specified that the system should look in C: and the box is not ticked, then the system will only look for files within C: and not within the many directories that C: contains. Figure 7.2a shows the results of a search for *config.sys*. In fact, the operational version is in the top level of C:, but the system has also found three other versions that are stored elsewhere on the system (probably part of the installation files). If the box had not been ticked, the result would have been as in Figure 7.2b.

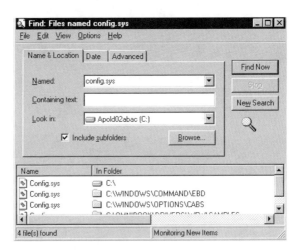

Figure 7.2a Results of search for '*config.sys*'.

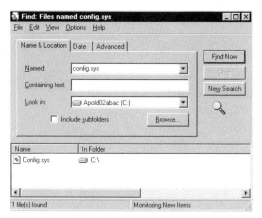

Figure 7.2b Results of search for *'config.sys'* **with Include subfolders box not ticked.**

If you do not know the full file name, you can enter any part of it and the system will find all those files with names that contain this string. Thus Figure 7.3a shows that just searching for *config* brings up many more results, while searching for *sys* (Figure 7.3b) brings up even more.

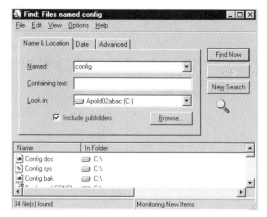

Figure 7.3a Results of search for 'config'.

To locate a folder or directory, you proceed in exactly the same way. Indeed, the search results will include both files and folders. These can be distinguished either by looking at the icon, or by nothing that folders/directories always end with a backslash. Note that if you select any file or folder and go to the **File** menu, clicking on **Open Containing Folder** will do just that, opening the folder containing the file or folder you have found.

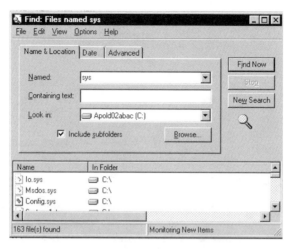

Figure 7.3b Results of search for '*sys*'.

Self Study

Try putting in partial file names of some of the common file extensions we looked at in Chapter 5. See what anomalies this may throw up.

7.4. Text Strings

Exercise 7.4

The second box, **Containing text**, in the **Find** window allows you to specify a text string that occurs within a file. Again you just type the string into the box. You can narrow down the range of directories and files where you want the system to search if you wish. Thus, say you write letters to someone called Jones and you store these in a directory called letters. You want to find all the references to Brown in letters to Jones (which you called jones01.doc, jones02.doc etc.). The search box would look like Figure 7.4 and note that the directories to be searched have automatically changed to Document Folders. However, this search would also throw up all files that include any occurrence of brown including, for example, the phrase 'brown shoes'. So, if, you go to the **Options** menu at the top of the **Find** window, you can choose **Case sensitive**, which means that if you enter *Brown* (rather than *brown*) in the **Containing text** box, you will only be given files in which Brown (with a capital B) appears. Of course, if 'Brown shoes' happens to appear at the beginning of a sentence, then the file containing that will appear as well, but case sensitivity does help in most cases.

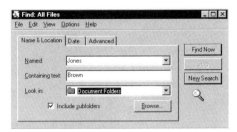

Figure 7.4 Example of search box.

caution!

Note that the case sensitivity option does not apply to file names, because, although Windows appears to allow case sensitivity in file names, it really does not, so Config.sys, CONFIG.SYS and config.sys all describe the same file. This is not really a problem, because Windows always warns you if you are in danger of overwriting a file with the same name.

Self Study

Add some text to the text box and try searching Help files (extension .hlp).

7.5. Date Options

Exercise 7.5

If you now select the **Date** tab in the **Find** window, you will see a window such as Figure 7.5. If you click on the white circle beside **Find all Files Modified**, then you can specify dates. Note that **Modified** is in a box and you can change it to **Created** or **Last accessed** by clicking the down arrow at the right-hand side of the box and selecting the appropriate option.

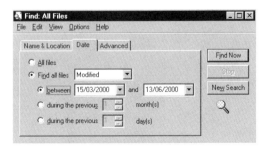

Figure 7.5 Specifying the date criteria when finding files.

★ ECDL ★

You can then put in specific dates (check which date convention your system is using – see Chapter 2 – or else you may confuse 5 March and 3 May, for example) or specify the period in months or days. This information works together with the information in the first tab. If you close **Find** and reopen it, you will find that it reverts to **All files**. However, if you leave **Find** open on your desktop and then come back to it later to carry out another search, there is nothing in the **Name & Location** tab to tell you that you narrowed the date range. It is worth checking this, or you may find that the search does not give you the result you want.

Self Study

Search for all the files you have modified in the last week and the last month.

7.6. Advanced Options

If you select the advanced tab (Figure7.6a), you will find that by using the top box, you can narrow your search to a certain type of file or folder. Just click the down arrow at the right-hand side of the **Of type** box (Figure 7.6b) to select a type.

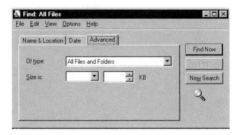

Figure 7.6a Using the Advanced tab for finding files.

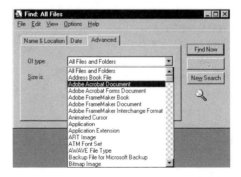

Fiugre 7.6b Selecting specific file or folder types.

You can also specify the maximum or minimum size of the file you are looking for.

These options can be used separately or together and are used in conjunction with settings in the first two tabs. Just as for the date, the settings are cancelled when you close Find, but, while the window is open, they remain in force, so you need to check them if you are coming back to reuse an open Find window.

Self Study

Take the same common file extensions that you used in the first exercise in this section and specify that type of file in the Advanced tab. See if you get similar results.

7.7. Saving Searches

If you go the **File** menu and select **Save search**, an icon will be created on your desktop. If you subsequently click on this, the search (with all its settings) will be updated. There may be times when this is useful, particularly if the search is fairly generic, such as find all files Modified in the last 7 days, but there is a danger of cluttering your desktop.

7.8. New Search

An important button is **New Search**. Clicking this will allow you to specify a new search. Note that if you click this, while it clears the settings in the Name & Location and the Advanced tabs, it does not clear the settings in the Date tab.

You will also see that the **Named** box has a down arrow on its right-hand side. If you click this, you will see the last nine entries in this box.

Summary

In this chapter:

- We have looked at the Find facility.
- We have examined the various options for specifying file names and text that is included in the file.
- We have looked at the date conditions that can be applied.
- We have looked at the file type conditions that can be applied.

Editing
Text Files

In this chapter you will learn how to

- *Launch an editing program or word processor.*
- *Open a file or create one and save it.*
- *Close the file and the application.*

8.1. Introduction

We have noted earlier the difference between text files and files normally generated by a word processor. The former contain just text, plus the carriage returns and tab characters, while the latter contain all kinds of formatting commands. So, although you can edit text files in a word processor, and we shall see how you do that, you do not actually need a word processor to edit them.

Windows provides you with a text editor, called Notepad, and a very basic word processor, called WordPad. However, for any serious word processing, you need to look at Microsoft Word (see Module 3) or a similar program, such as WordPerfect or WordPro. Here, however, we shall simply look at Notepad and WordPad.

8.2. Opening a File in Notepad and WordPad

If you want to edit a text file, which will usually have the extension .txt (although there are other files that are also text files, e.g. .ini and .bat files), when you click to open it in My Computer or in Windows Explorer, you will find that it will most probably open in Notepad (see Figure 8.1), which you can see is very basic. Notepad has a limit on the length of the file it can open, so you will sometimes see a message that tells you that the file you want to open is too large for Notepad and asks you if you would like to use WordPad instead.

Figure 8.1 The Notepad text editor.

Exercise 8.2

Alternatively, if you want to open Notepad directly, you go to **Start** and select **Programs**. Then open **Accessories**, which is usually the first item shown, and then choose **Notepad**. Incidentally, you will see that **WordPad** is opened in the same way; it is lower down the list of accessories. Once you have opened Notepad, try keying a few paragraphs of text. Alternatively, you can try opening a file with the extension .txt.

8.3. Using Notepad to Edit and Create Files

Even Notepad has a few formatting features in case you want to print a file.

Exercise 8.3

If you open the **File** menu, you will see that you can choose **Page Setup**, which allows you to specify the size and orientation of paper and the margins; printing is dealt with in Chapter 9. Note that the formatting is not stored with the file.

The **Edit** menu has the usual **Cut**, **Copy** and **Paste** and **Select All** that we have seen in previous sections. Here, however, if you use select, then you select strings or blocks of text and, if you cut or copy, you cut or copy the text you have selected; similarly with paste. Try this with the file that you created or opened in Exercise 8.2.

The other two entries in the **Edit** menu that are of interest are **Time/Date**, which inserts the system time and date into the file, and **Word Wrap**, which, if switched on, wraps the lines (i.e. inserts temporary carriage returns) so that they all fit within the editing window. If Word Wrap is switched off and there are only carriage returns at the end of each paragraph, you will only see the first few words of each paragraph in your editing window. You can, of course, use the horizontal scroll bar, just like the ones we saw in Chapter 2, but if the text wraps it makes reading much simpler. **Search** allows you to look for sequences of letters and is self-explanatory.

If you already have a file open in Notepad, you can make any changes by adding or deleting characters using the keyboard. In fact, in many ways you can think of Notepad as rather like an electronic typewriter. Once you have finished your editing, you can save the file, either directly by using **Save** in the **File** menu, when your new version will overwrite the old version, or you can use **Save As**, in which case you either give the file a new name or you save it under the same name (or a new name) in a new directory (Figure 8.2).

In this way your original file is preserved. Saving to a diskette simply involves browsing through the system until you find the diskette letter (usually A:, but occasionally B:). Then you just save in the usual way, ensuring, of course, that you have the right diskette in the drive.

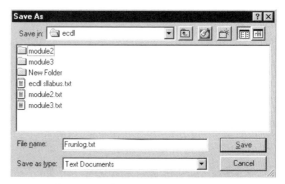

Figure 8.2 Saving a Notepad file.

Note that you can only have one file open at a time in Notepad, so if you go to **File** and then select **Open** or **New**, you will be asked if you want to save any changes to the file that is currently open. Note that if you have not made any changes, you will not see this message. To open a file, key open and you will see a window (Figure 8.3) that is rather like the My Computer window and not unlike the Save As menu. You can browse in this until you find the file you want, which you open by selecting it and then clicking on **Open** or by double clicking.

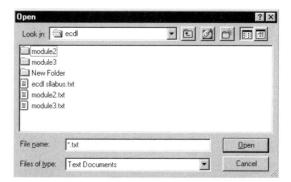

Figure 8.3 Opening a file in Notepad.

If you want to create a new file, you select **New** in the **File** menu and the window will go blank and the file name **Untitled** will appear in the window title bar. Again you just type in the window and, when you are ready to save, you select **Save** from the **File** menu. You will see a window that is very like

the Save As window and you can browse to decide where you want to save the file and type in the name you want to use. Note that if you leave the box **Save as Type** showing **Text documents**, the system will automatically add the .txt extension for you.

Self Study

Find a text file on your system (use Find, as described in Section 7). Open it in Notepad. Switch on word wrap if you can only see the beginnings of lines. Do not make any changes. Click Save As in the File menu and save under a name in your ECDL directory. Then select New in the File menu and open a new file. Type something into it, but do not save. Select New again and see what message you get. It is up to you whether you save what you have done.

8.4. Using WordPad to Edit and Create Files

The WordPad window is shown in Figure 8.4. Although WordPad allows you to format files, setting the typeface (font), typesize and various aspects of layout, such as bullets, if you are editing a text file, then these things are irrelevant because when you save the file they are lost. However, what WordPad does allow you to do (as indeed does Word) is open a file formatted in Word or one that is in the Rich Text Format (RTF) and save it as a text file. To balance this, you can save a text file as a Word document. You also have the page setup controls that you find in Notepad and again, unlike a fully featured word processor, the page setup is not retained as part of the file when you save it.

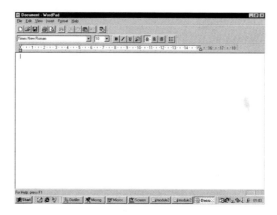

Figure 8.4 The WordPad window.

107

To open a file, select **Open** from the **File** menu and you will see a window like that shown in Figure 8.5, where the file type drop-down list is shown. You select the type of file you want to open and these will be displayed. You also need to browse until you find the appropriate directory. If you open a Word file, it will appear formatted (Figure 8.6), while a text file will be unformatted and the formatting bar will disappear (Figure 8.7). However, you can add formatting using the Format menu and then save as a Word file (with a file extension of .doc) and the formatting bar will reappear.

Figure 8.5 Opening a file in WordPad.

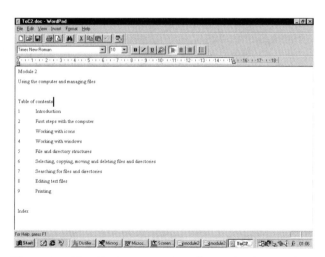

Figure 8.6 WordPad opens Word files with formatting.

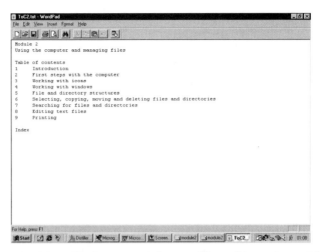

Figure 8.7 WordPad opens plain text files without formatting.

Similarly, if you open a Word file and save it as a text file, the formatting bar will disappear, although the formatting will remain on the screen. However, if you close WordPad (and WordPad is like Notepad in that you can only close the file by closing the application, opening another file or creating a new file) and then reopen the text file in WordPad, the formatting will have gone. You use **Save** and **Save As** in exactly the same way as you would with Notepad.

You may find that using WordPad gives you a simple introduction to word processors, because it is much simpler than Word. In practice, it is generally only used to edit text files that are too large for Notepad.

Self Study

Repeat the first exercise in this chapter, but try adding some formatting to your new file and saving it as a Word file.

8.5. Closing Notepad or WordPad

As already noted, both these applications can only have one file open at a time. Thus, closing the file means closing the application, while opening another file means closing the current file.

To close either application, go to the **File** menu and select **Exit**. If you have unsaved changes in the current file, you will be asked if you want to save the file. Otherwise, it will simply exit.

Summary

In this chapter:

- We have looked at editing text files in Notepad.
- We have looked at editing text and Word files in WordPad.

Printing

In this chapter you will learn how to

- *Carry out printing.*
- *Change the default printer.*
- *View the progress of a print job.*

9.1. Introduction

Even in this age of electronic communication, it is more than likely that you will need a printed version of a file you have been working on. Windows is able to store details of many printers and you can switch between them if they are attached to your system. However, there is always a default printer, which is the one to which documents are automatically sent unless you indicate otherwise.

In practice, most printing is done from within applications, so just as we saw in the last chapter that you can use the Print command from the File menu of Notepad or WordPad, so virtually every application, including Web browsers, has a Print command on its File menu.

On the other hand it is possible to print directly from a desktop window if a file has an application associated with it. Strictly speaking, however, the associated application opens and moves straight to printing. If there is no associated application, the Print option does not appear on the File menu.

9.2. Printing from a Desktop Window

If you select a file using **My Computer** and then select **Print** from the **File** menu, you will see that the application which is associated with that file will open and the file will be printed immediately by the default printer. If there is no associated application, then Print does not appear on the File menu.

9.3. Printing from Within an Application

Exactly how print works within an application, i.e. exactly what options you see to print all the pages, some of the pages, left-hand pages, right-hand pages etc., varies from application to application. Notepad, for example, gives you no options and prints directly, while WordPad is rather more complex and not untypical of many applications. When you select **Print**, you see the menu shown in Figure 9.1. This allows you to choose which printer to use (the one that is shown initially is the default printer), how many copies to print (and how to collate them). If you click on **Properties**, you see another window (Figure 9.2), which varies depending on the printer; each printer has its own driver software, which determines what you see here. What always appears, however, is the option to change the paper size (you may find that many applications use the US letter size as default, so you need to change to A4) and the orientation of the page on the printer, that is, portrait (long side vertical) or landscape (long side horizontal). Once you have made your selection, click **OK** and then again **OK** in the main printer window.

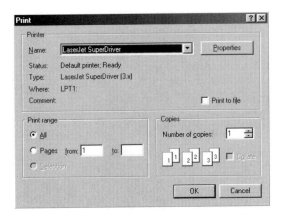

Figure 9.1 Dialogue for selecting printer.

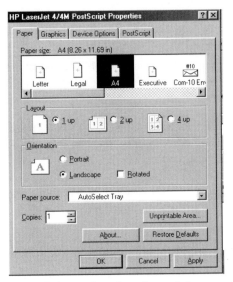

Figure 9.2 Dialogue for choosing print properties.

9.4. Changing the Default Printer

Exercise 9.4

As noted above, the system always has a default printer, but you can change this:

step **1.** Go to **Start** and select **Settings** and then **Printers**. A window will open
that looks like Figure 9.3. Exactly how it will look will depend on your
particular system.

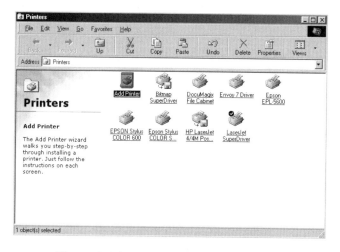

Figure 9.3 Changing the default printer.

step **2.** Select the printer you want to make the default. (Perhaps you have changed
your printer or want to run a long job on a printer that is currently not the
default.) Note that you can add printers to this folder if required.

step **3.** Go to the **File** menu and select **Set as Default** (or right click on the printer
icon and select **Set as Default** from the menu that appears). If there is a
tick alongside this, then this printer is already the default printer.

step **4.** Close the Printers window. The next time you print from an application, it will
be your new default printer that will appear in the options window.

9.5. Viewing the Progress of Printing

If you have sent a number of documents to be printed, you may wish
to review their progress. You can do this from the desktop print
manager. There are two ways to do this.

Exercise 9.5

step **1.** Open the Printers window (**Start/Settings/Printers**) and then select the
printer you are currently using and open it. You will see a window like that in
Figure 9.4, which shows you the progress of the various print jobs you have
sent to this printer.

★ ★ ★
★ ★
★ ECDL ★
★ ★
★ ★

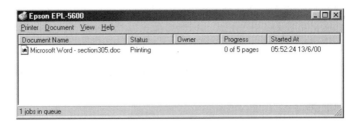

Figure 9.4 Progress of print jobs.

step **2.** When you start to print, you will see a printer icon open in the Taskbar at the bottom right of your screen (next to the time in most cases). If you click on this, you will see the same window as in Figure 9.4. The icon will remain as long as there are files being printed. When printing is complete, it will disappear.

information

> **From the print manager screen, you can also pause or purge printing. This can be useful if, for example, you have a long print queue and suddenly have something urgent to print or if the printer jams and you need to stop printing.**

Summary

In this chapter:

- We have seen how to print from a desktop window and from within an application.
- We have seen how to change the default printer.
- We have seen how to review the progress of printing.

Index

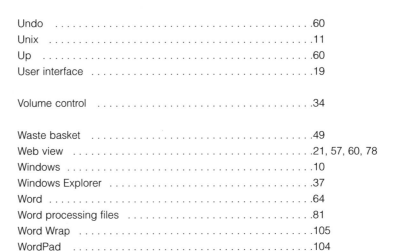

European Computer Driving Licence™

the european pc skills standard

Springer's study guides have been designed to complement the ECDL syllabus, and be consistent with the content contained within it. Each study guide enables you to successfully complete the European Driving Licence (ECDL). The books cover a range of specific knowledge areas and skill sets, with clearly defined learning objectives, broken down into seven modules.

Each module has been written in clear, jargon-free language, with self-paced exercises and regular review questions, to help prepare you for ECDL Tests.

Titles in the series include:

- **Module 1: Basic Concepts of Information Technology**
  ISBN: 1-85233-442-8   Softcover   £9.95

- **Module 2: Using the Computer & Managing Files**
  ISBN: 1-85233-443-6   Softcover   £9.95

- **Module 3: Word Processing**
  ISBN: 1-85233-444-4   Softcover   £9.95

- **Module 4: Spreadsheets**
  ISBN: 1-85233-445-2   Softcover   £9.95

- **Module 5: Database**
  ISBN: 1-85233-446-0   Softcover   £9.95

- **Module 6: Presentation**
  ISBN: 1-85233-447-9   Softcover   £9.95

- **Module 7: Information & Communication**
  ISBN: 1-85233-448-7   Softcover   £9.95

All books are available, of course, from all good booksellers (who can order them even if they are not in stock), but if you have difficulties you can contact the publisher direct by telephoning +44 (0) 1483 418822 or by emailing orders@svl.co.uk

For details of other Springer books and journals, please visit

www.springer.de